Julie de Lespinasse

The Salon

A Study of French Society and Personalities
in the Eighteenth Century

By

Helen Clergue

Illustrated

G. P. Putnam's Sons
New York and London
The Knickerbocker Press
1907

The Knickerbocker Press, New York

To

Edward Stanley Roscoe

But for whose advice and encouragement this book
would not have been written.

PREFACE

THE object of these studies is to indicate the part which the salon has played in the history of French society. I have endeavoured to illustrate this by the presentment of four typical women and, in the preliminary study, to describe some of the most striking features of a part of French society, so that the reader may appreciate the world into which those whose lives are here sketched were born and its effect upon them. The whole is intended to show how the feminine element, which has been so important an influence in the development of modern society, was at work in eighteenth-century France.

The four women who have been selected as types lived in the same period and, between them, may be said to embody the different phases of the Parisian society of their day. No two persons could well be in

greater contrast than exclusive, aristocratic
Madame Du Deffand, and bourgeoise, philanthropic Madame Geoffrin, her rival. Julie
de Lespinasse and Madame d' Épinay illustrate the gentler and more feminine types of
character. The former united in her salon
the prominent features which characterised
the societies of Madame Du Deffand and
of Madame Goeffrin, borrowing its critical
features from that of the earlier friend, and
its philosophical element from the later. The
salon of Madame d'Épinay was the more
purely philosophical, and association with
Rousseau during the most mentally active
period of his life, undoubtedly influenced her
moral theories.

Madame Du Deffand, in whose salon is
seen, in the greatest degree, a survival
of seventeenth-century ideas, may be said
to represent pure intellect, Julie de Lespinasse, who would be extraordinary in any
age, unquenchable, uncontrollable passion.
Madame d'Épinay and Madame Geoffrin
whose lives demonstrate, the one, the order
of morals, the other, the democratic tend-

encies of this epoch, correspond more exactly to it and are its more representative products.

That the ethical view-point of the age in which they live must be understood in judging historical characters is an axiom which, though it should be obvious to the student, is often not clear to the general reader, and a few words perhaps may not be out of place to emphasise the ethical attitude which a reader of to-day should take toward those women who directed the salons.

There is a general idea in English-speaking countries that they were all women without moral principle, and any study of them is usually undertaken with this preconceived prejudice. On the contrary, though living in a lax and licentious age, they essentially assisted in raising its moral tone, and the radical changes effected by the Revolution, which altered the structure of society, and to which its rapid ethical advance is owing, had their birth, and were fostered, in the salon.

The personality, lives, and social adventures of those who have popularly been called the women of the salons are always interesting, but these features have been dwelt upon, perhaps, to excess. We are apt to forget in reading of their careers that they illustrate the age and its influences—that they may be studied and analysed, not only from a psychological, but also from an historical point of view and in connection with the tendencies and currents of the times—in other words, that they are not mere isolated figures.

I take this opportunity to thank the Hon. Arthur D. Elliot for his continuous encouragement. I must also thank the publishers of the *Edinburgh Review* for permission to include in this volume the studies on Madame Du Deffand, Madame d'Épinay, and Julie de Lespinasse which originally appeared, for the most part, in its pages. And I wish to express my deep sense of obligation to the late Madame Th. Blanc-Benthzon. To her I am indebted for valuable unpublished material; and my intercourse with her during the final preparation of these studies added much to the pleasure of my work.

April, 1907.   HELEN CLERGUE.

CONTENTS

ILLUSTRATIONS

xi

Illustrations

"Ce siècle, chose étrange, a été jusqu' ici dédaigné par l'histoire. Ils semblent qu' ils aient craint d'être notés de légèreté en s'approchant de ce siècle dont la légèreté n'est que la surface et le masque."

E. AND J. DE GONCOURT.

The Salon

I

THE salon of the eighteenth century was not a mere accidental social phenomenon ; it was the natural result, not only of a concurrence of various remarkable phases in society as it existed in that changing period, but of ideas the germs of which were in active movement in the Middle Ages.

The mediæval woman of chivalry was conceded to be a being of finer material than the man, however powerful or brave, and her supremacy was essentially spiritual for, in the songs of chivalry, the knight invariably endowed his lady with superior qualities of mind and heart. These chivalric ideas, generated in Provence, took root in the fruitful soil of Italy. Cities have ever offered the most favourable environment for intellectual women, and it is in the rich and cultivated centres of the Italian renaissance, that loved beauty and learning, and contained exceptional women, such as Michael Angelo's friend, the poet Vittoria Colonna who brought together the great and wise, that the salon, which raised the scholar to the level of the noble, finds its precursor.

But the union of birth and learning in the formation of society in Italy was of a sporadic nature only, and the movement did not obtain a recognised value until the seventeenth century opened, when an important change took place and a marked advance was made in European thought. The centre of learning and culture shifted from Italy to France, and clever women of the highest rank then, for the first time, invited the scholars to meet the nobles on an equal footing, and scholars studied manners and nobles' wit.

As early as the sixteenth century Mar-

guerite de Valois[1] had brought together
at her remarkable court in Navarre the
elements which later developed into the
salon, but the position which women took
and maintained with the opening of the
hôtel de Rambouillet in 1617—that of bringing together diverse elements in society and
keeping them entirely submissive to their
will and pleasure—gave women a wholly
new and distinct power and influence, a
place gained and maintained neither as
women of letters nor politicians, but by the
feminine qualities of tact, sympathy, and
mental alertness.

This novel supremacy of women in Paris,
which involved a recognition alike of intellectual attributes and of feminine charm,
was contemporaneous with an inferior status
in other parts of Europe where women were
hardly more than slaves among the peas-
ants, mere housewives among the middle
class, and propagators of the race, or toys,
among the aristocracy. That which made
the position of the French woman the more
remarkable was that it occurred in a country

[1] Marguerite de Valois-Angoulême, château d'Odos.

where her situation in regard to marriage and family life was, and has largely remained, one of subservience to the head of the family; not as in England, where individual freedom had already become a constitutional maxim.

In England, too, no such social products as Madame Geoffrin and Julie de Lespinasse were ever to be seen, though the salon in France was not without influence on English society. But the attempts of women like Mrs. Montagu to obtain in London a position such as that of Madame Geoffrin in Paris were generally regarded as eccentricities, even if the Englishwoman's breakfast parties were crowded. Not only society as it existed in France, but qualities peculiar to the French woman were necessary for the maintenance of a salon.

In no other country have men and women become the intellectual companions that they have in France, a state of society dating from the ascendency of the salon. The same subjects may be discussed, and in the same detached and impersonal manner, between

men and women as among men alone.
The mental freedom and development
affected by this intellectual comradeship
has given to the French woman a masculine
breadth of view not to be found elsewhere.

But this alone would not insure success
in the career to which these women aspired,
and to feminine insight and the ready and
clear intelligence which is a mental attribute
of their race they necessarily united gifts of
character; necessarily, for a vain woman
would inevitably have failed in such an undertaking. The first aim of the leader of
a salon was to make others shine rather
than to attract attention to herself. Nor
was vanity encouraged in any member of
the circle, for the hostess skilfully directed
and manipulated the conversation, tossing it,
as her ready wits suggested, from one to another. The topic, and the manner of treating
it, was entirely subject to her control and,
no matter how burning the question under
discussion might be, nor how much the company might differ concerning it, no exhibition
of ill-will or undue excitement was ever for

a moment tolerated, gentle manners were as indispensable as clear brains.

As late as the seventeenth century women were of scarcely any social, and of less political, importance ; it was the opening of the salon of the Marquise de Rambouillet in Paris that marked their advent as accepted social factors. Henceforth a sufficiently able and ambitious woman, forced no longer as she grew older to take refuge within the cloister from neglect and want of occupation, might, instead of repressing the activity of her mind, exercise it by forming a congenial society.

The history of the salon proper begins with that of the Marquise de Rambouillet who herself designed and adorned the magnificent hôtel de Rambouillet, where she gathered together a company which exercised a marked and happy influence on literature and manners, where the standing of men of letters was raised and assured, where noblemen turned to study and refined pleasures, and where women were recognised as intellectual companions for men.

The salon of Madame de Rambouillet, by its radical alteration of the relations ① between men and women as well as between conditions, radically affected also the ② course of French letters. The influence which women with the opening of the hôtel de Rambouillet exerted on literature is, indeed, incalculable. "The theatre of Corneille expresses the ideal of the hôtel de Rambouillet," says Brunetière; the salons also, he writes,

were opened to writers at an epoch, and even at the precise time when one might have asked, not without some anxiety, if literature were not degenerating with the school of Mathurin Regnier, for example, into a species of Bohemianism;—they directed the observation of dramatic authors and of romantic writers toward the analysis or the anatomy of that passion of love which will be always, whatever may be said, the material preferred in romantic or poetic fiction; and from this anatomy of the passion of love, they attempted to outline the struggles of conscience, rules of conduct, and an ideal of life which governed even the other passions too.[1]

Whilst admitting that the superiority in style which the French possesses over

[1] *Les Philosophes et la Société Française,* par M. Ferdinand Brunetière, *Revue des Deux Mondes,* 1er Dec., 1906, p. 619.

other literatures was due to the influence of women in the salon, Brunetière considered that their influence impoverished literature by making it aristocratic, thus preventing it from becoming popular. He claimed, too, that the very perfection which the language attained in its form tended to uniformity; that form was gained at the cost of originality. This criticism more nearly concerns the seventeenth century, whose greatest writers, Molière, Pascal, and Boileau, were hostile to the salon, than to the eighteenth, when the intellectual activity of the salon, at the height of its power, had become political in its effects and men's minds were finally engrossed with serious constitutional changes. Not one great writer in the eighteenth century but submitted to the influence of the salon, derived sustenance from it, and composed for it. Montesquieu left his vines to visit Madame de Lambert and Madame de Tencin, Voltaire was a frequenter of the salons and intimate with their most influential leaders, the genius of Rousseau developed under the roof provided by Ma-

dame d' Épinay, Buffon's powerful will bent
before Madame Necker, and the hitherto
untamed Diderot regretted, on her account,
the grossness of his writings.

It is owing to the salon, no doubt, that
" serious questions were treated wittily and
bagatelles seriously,"[1] but the epoch of
literature cannot be said to be wanting
in seriousness, or in breadth, force, or
originality, which could produce such men
as these.[2]

The original members of the French Academy were recognised as the most distinguished guests at the hôtel de Rambouillet,
and, following Ronsard and the Pléïade,
they met with every encouragement in their
task of reconstructing the language.   In this
hotel Bossuet improvised his first sermon,
and intimately connected with the renowned
structure are the names of La Rochefoucauld
and the Comtesse de La Fayette—roman-
tically intertwined—Corneille, the Marquise

[1] Brunetière, *Manuel de l'Histoire de la Littérature Française*,
Paris, 1907, p. 339.

[2] *Les Philosophes et la Société Française du XVIIIme Siècle*,
par Marius Roustan, Paris et Lyon, 1906, p. 258.

de Sévigné, the Duchesse de Longueville, Mademoiselle de Scudéry, the Marquise de Sablé, and the Duchesse de Montpensier— the Grande Mademoiselle—several of whom, after the death of Madame de Rambouillet, opened their own salons, where was continued the revolutionary propaganda in the world of thought.   Despite the fact that authorship for women was tabooed in society, Mademoiselle de Scudéry and Madame de La Fayette also, gave vent to their ideas, and to their regrets, desires, and dreams, in long romances; but, admired as it was, Madame de La Fayette disclaimed all knowledge of her celebrated work, the *Princesse de Clèves.* Of such was the brilliant company to be found in the exquisite " chambre bleu " of the Marquise de Rambouillet, a salon which, in its constructive power, in its elegance and its refinement, was never equalled.

Considering the slow and painful growth which attends the common course of events, this, the first of the salons, is seen to be an extraordinary product; a vision singularly perfect and homogeneous, it issues from the

mists of the past. But we are regarding
the dawn of the most brilliant period of
French history; the grand siècle is in
progress.

As I have said, it was in the eighteenth
century that the salon obtained its greatest
influence. The Marquise de Lambert, born
in 1646, who established the most noteworthy salon of the first half of the eighteenth century, lived in a time when she
could catch a reflection, at least, from
the declining glory of the hôtel de Rambouillet and, before its final extinction,
could hear it familiarly discussed. A woman of the highest intelligence, fond of
study and reflection, Madame de Lambert
was quick to grasp the meaning of this new
conception of society, but it was not until the
later years of her life that she ventured upon
a ground where wide experience, ripe judgment, and knowledge of men were required
to walk without stumbling in the path broken
by Madame de Rambouillet. Not only did
Madame de Lambert successfully compete
with her predecessors but her salon connected

and, in a manner, united the two periods in which she lived, for, upholding the decorum and moderation and containing the critical tone which marked the salon of the seventeenth century, it conceived, also, the generous theories which led to the philosophical and political movement of the eighteenth century.

Madame de Lambert was a rich widow of uncommon attainments, chiefly owing to the education she had received from Bachaumont, her step-father, when, in 1710, she opened her salon in the Palais Mazarin—the only existing wing of which was built by her—the culminating point in a life which had been hitherto by no means either empty or uneventful. The signal example which had been set by the Marquise de Rambouillet was closely followed by Madame de Lambert, and the same high ethical standard imposed amid the license which surrounded the court of Henri IV, was upheld in the far worse case of the Regent.

One of the phases which mark the advance of the modern spirit to be seen in the salon was the support given candidates to the French academy. The name of Madame de Rambouillet, the founder of the salon, is inseparably connected with the founding of the French Academy, and this institution was closely associated thereafter with the salons, gathering its recruits, without interruption, from one or another. Madame de Lambert actively and openly electioneered for her candidates, and is said to have made half the Academicians of her time, her salon being called the "ante-chamber" of the Academy, a term repeated in respect to the salon of Julie de Lespinasse.

II

There are other characteristics which, throughout its history, follow the course of the salon. There was little card playing, the common fashionable dissipation, and music entered into its composition chiefly as a topic of conversation. The tête-à-tête was prohibited, and subjects were discussed in common. Should any one suppose he had reason to be given more attention than another, he was quickly disillusioned for he must soon discover that, instead of attention being directed to him, he was only expected to add his ideas to the subject under discussion. D'Alembert, admirable talker though he was, was never permitted to monopolise the conversation, even in the salon of his dear friend, Julie de Lespinasse. Conversation can never be general where there are many people ; consequently the number received at one time was never large ; it was conversation which was the fundamental, and which was uniformly maintained as the chief, feature of the salon.

Julie de Lespinasse, writing to Condorcet, complained that as both Turgot and the Duchesse d'Enville wrote him every day, it was difficult to find news to tell him. It must be acknowledged that the habitués often felt the need of exchanging ideas; every day, or even twice a day, was not too often, and if it were impossible to see one another, the hiatus was filled by long letters.

what?

Interchanges of ideas cause their diffusion, and the learned, in answer to the crying need for the wider distribution of knowledge, began to forsake their Latin and to write in the popular tongue. Science as well as literature was thus brought within the comprehension of the general public, Fontenelle, for example, substituting French for Latin, and simple terms for scientific formulæ— thereby producing his best and most useful work—in order that Madame de Lambert might be able to read his scientific treatises. The Academicians wrought over the French language, forming and perfecting it in the Palais Mazarin, just as they had done in the hôtel de Rambouillet. Women did not then publish their writings, but Madame de Lambert wrote—chiefly on education—with a care which suggests expectation of a larger audience than that of her children, for whom her productions were ostensibly designed.

Her style is clear and unaffected, and her ideas are advanced. Some of her sayings contain, it is true, a certain worldly wisdom which is suggestive of Lord Chesterfield's

calculating advice to his son, but her code
of ethics is higher. A woman of deep feeling, she saw the danger which lies in the
ascendency of the emotions. "We should
fear great emotions of the soul, which pre-
pare ennui and disgust. . . . We become so accustomed to ardent pleasures
that we cannot fall back upon simple ones,"
she wrote. "Very respectable," was the
satirical designation with which some of the
wits sought to cast ridicule upon the high
character of her society, but their efforts
were attended with no better results than
had been obtained by those who attempted
to identify the ridiculous features of the
Précieuses with the hôtel de Rambouillet.
Through Madame de Lambert and her salon,
Madame de Sevigné is linked with her epistolary prototype of a later century, Madame
Du Deffand, and Madame de Rambouillet,
refined and aspiring, with Madame de Tencin, clever and corrupt, for after Madame de
Lambert, the character of the salon percep-
tibly changes.

The ethics of an age have been well

described as the "common conscience" of its own civilisation. They are determined by various, often conflicting, causes, sometimes by the good or bad example of a court or aristocracy, sometimes by the levelling process of democracy, again by impalpable forces which cannot be grasped, and the salon, which was the certain index of its time, instantly betrayed their least variation. "Opinion," said Voltaire, "governs the world." And the salons governed opinion; but the women who directed them were, after Madame de Lambert, themselves no longer guided by the same ideals which had inspired those who had evolved the seventeenth-century salon. Romance and sentiment were ridiculed, and ridicule was feared like the plague.[1] Marriage merely opened a door to freedom and pleasure for women, and neither party to the contract expected the least constraint to be placed on his or her desires beyond that required by taste, which was the real and only ethical

[1] *Julie*, J.-J. Rousseau.   Paris: Garnier Frères, p. 196.

2

governor, for eighteenth-century society never lost its respect for fine manners. *Bon-ton* was the definition society gave to taste; the phrase signified ease in conversation, politeness in expression, respect to persons, regard for appearances, a manner which confounded neither condition, place, nor persons, a tact which equally advised the respect due to others and to oneself. And, moreover, no man dared disregard, and no project could hope to succeed without the sanction of, *bon-ton*.[1]

III

As the eighteenth century advanced spiritual aspiration gave place to materialism, the spirit of repose to restlessness, anxiety, and excitement. Science arose; natural history, history, sociology, political economy, had their birth in the eighteenth century. Faith declined; there were those who even reproached Voltaire as "bigot" and " deist"; but an attempt was made to fill the religious

[1] Mademoiselle de Sommery. Quoted by Grimm. *Correspondance Littéraire*, 17 tomes en 3 parties, Paris, 1812, 1813, 1814, troisième partie, t. 11, p. 125.

void by the teaching of an ethical philosophy
and by the practice of an altruistic cult
which went by the name of humanity.

Material as are many of its phases, the
eighteenth century is too often condemned,
in its totality, by the moralist, as a de-
cadent age. Like all epochs it possesses
its transitional features when the forms
of one are to be seen intermingled with
those of another; the century may, however, be divided into three periods, each
of which is quite different in character to
the others. The first, when the influence
of the seventeenth century still lingered, was
epitomised in the dignified, tranquil, and
constructive salon of Madame de Lambert.
The second, or middle period, was the licentious age, fitly exemplified in the life of
Madame de Tencin. While the third, which
ushered in the Revolution, was a time of
travail and of regeneration. This third period,
as it draws towards its close, may be styled
a particularly moral epoch when we consider its substitution of generosity and self-
sacrifice for worldliness and prudence,

enthusiasm for coldness, its return to many of the fundamental duties of every-day life; its hatred of injustice, sham, and affectation, and its diligent search after truth. It is plain that the ethical view-point has again undergone a radical change.

As the Revolution draws near, birth, which formerly had condescended to intellect, is now seen to be losing ground ; intellectual predominance becomes more marked, while the authority of the well born, as such, is felt to be rapidly waning.

The power and the usefulness of the salons were due to one particular cause : they were intellectual exchanges. The literary and philosophical salon, where mental activity was most pronounced, and where discussion was freest, gained continually over the fashionable hôtel. The ambitious Duchesse de Maine with her little court at Sceaux; the powerful Maréchale de Luxembourg at her magnificent château of Montmorency ; the amiable Princesse de Beauvau, all of whom kept open houses— in spite of rank and riches—could never

MADAME DE TENCIN.
From an Engraving by J. C. Armytage.

compete, in power and in influence, with bourgeoise Madame Geoffrin, Julie de Lespinasse, the penniless outcast, or with Madame d'Épinay, whose fame waxed greater as her possessions grew less.

The début of the Marquise de Tencin, about 1729, in the character of the leader of a salon, emphasised the first change in the ethics of the eighteenth century. The reproach " very respectable " could never have been applied to her, though from this time the objectionable features of her life were laid aside ; but any woman who had borne such a reputation for intrigue, no matter how clever, could never, in the previous century, have succeeded in collecting such a remarkable group as she did about her.

On the death of Madame de Tencin, in 1749, the salons diverge and, as they increase, take on individual characteristics. For their numbers grow until, on the eve of the Revolution, when men's minds were made still more active by the prevailing excitement, a man looked up to like d'Alembert, or a popular foreigner like Horace Walpole, could, if he liked, divide the days of the week between different salons, in any one of which he would find a varied society, and mental stimulus. Madame Du Deffand, Julie de Lespinasse, Madame Geoffrin, Madame d'Épinay, Madame Necker, lived and ruled at one and the same time.

The forces which finally resulted in the Revolution were at this time drawing towards their culmination in every section of the social structure, and their action was visible in strangely unexpected places. It could be seen in the salons of Paris, as in the sumptuous apartments of the châteaux de La Chevrette and at Chantilly, and in those magnificent buildings which, surviving the Revolution, still rise in splendour high above the banks of the Loire and the Seine, and whose turrets and battlements peep out from Normandy forests or crown the heights in wild Périgord and savage Savoy. Courtiers, philosophers, and agreeable and clever women were here collected, whose discussions, animated by a spirit of criticism and inquiry, were destructive of these very surroundings.

IV

A salon, in the historical sense of the term, was neither a house which was always open to the world at large, nor did it at all resemble the modern day-reception in English-speaking countries, with its jumble of heterogeneous elements. It was a carefully selected and assorted company, its numbers regulated, and so skilfully arranged and directed as to form a homogeneous unity.

The salons are sometimes dwelt upon as a light and loose society, whose leaders and frequenters, freeing themselves not only from the restraints of conventionality, but from any standard of morality as well, carried freedom of speech to the extreme of license ; where an assemblage of dissipated, if brilliant, men were often gathered together by a frivolous and unconventional, probably equally censurable, though gifted, woman. Such was not the case. Great changes in

morals and in public sentiment generally
have occurred since their time, with the
gradual progress of civilisation and ideas,
and the world of to-day would be offended
at much which at that period was over-
looked or condoned; but the salon, far
from being an aid or abettor to a scandalous
life was, rather, society's adjuster—the
court of public opinion from whence there
was no appeal—as to behaviour and manners, while it inspired and directed the intelligence. (A high ideal of truth and beauty
was its constant aim) a perfect proportion, an exquisite harmony, which tended
to unity and temperance, was the rule, and
less freedom in the sense of license was to
be found there than in any society in the
great capitals of the world before or after;
therein lay its power and its success,
stimulating and enlarging, as it did, the
life of the intellect. The private life of the
individual, past or present, might be as corrupt as his code allowed, but when he entered the society of the salon, he must
satisfy the requirements of his environment

if he would remain. Here that which was best in thought and expression flourished, here all that was exalted in sentiment was applauded; and here, if an original idea were introduced, the divine spark was not permitted to expire for want of fanning. It is thus evident that the leader of a salon had no light task to perform; he or she was an arbiter accepted by society in the interest of good manners and high thinking, and any one who violated a law was peremptorily banished, for the ruler was autocratic and all-powerful.

The important salons were generally directed by women who were either unmarried, or widows, or women who did not live with their husbands; to prove, however, that it was possible for a husband to enter into their construction, there are the examples of the salons of Madame d'Holbach and Madame Helvétius, where husband and wife were both prominent. But women were not only the skilful hostesses, they were also— though men predominated—to be seen mingled in various types of elegance and

eloquence among the guests, and again, absolute as was the rule of the mistress of a salon,
not one but had its male presiding genius.
Madame Du Deffand and Président Hénault;
Grimm and Madame d'Épinay; these names
cannot be disassociated. The figure of
d'Alembert is always to be seen by the side
of Julie de Lespinasse, and Fontenelle was
the chief support and the leading *bel esprit*
in three successive salons.

The philosophy of the eighteenth century
has been called "the intellectual form of
the French Revolution." It should have
a special definition, for it possessed a special
and a new significance. The principle of
the sovereignty of reason dominated this
philosophy and was the bond of union uniting a multitudinous and confused mass of
theories accepted by men of otherwise contrary beliefs, and it was the authority of the
Church rather than that of the monarchy
against which this principle was directed.
The salon of the seventeenth century reformed manners, raised the status of men of
letters, and gave its precise and lucid style

to French literature ; in the eighteenth, it
converted society to the new ideas which
had been there evolved. The names of
those who subscribed to the *Encyclopédie*
were the great names of France, and beside
the nobles there are those of abbés, magis-
trates, stewards, governors, and financiers.[1]
Many of them, after the example of the Duc
de la Rochefoucauld, joyfully despoiled
themselves for these ideas, in the first epoch
of the Revolution, and some, like Rochefoucauld's cousin, the Duc de Liancourt,
remained faithful to them even throughout
the excesses of the Revolution, and, in assisting to raise a new social structure on its
ruins, were still true to the new philosophy.
It is one of the ironies of history that the
Revolution, which the intellectual activity of
the salon so greatly assisted, should be the
cause of its downfall, for the salon reached the
highest point of its development immediately
prior to the Revolution, and the last half of
the century saw its apogee and its decline.

[1] *Les Philosophes et la Société Française au XVIIIme Siècle*, par
Marius Roustan, Lyon et Paris, 1906, pp. 2 and 250.

There have been salons since; Madame de Staël's disconnected life, driven though she was from pillar to post by Napoleon, could not debar a career which was, with her, an inheritance; and Madame Récamier, her contemporary and friend, though so inferior from an intellectual standpoint, had one of the most renowned and successful social careers in history; the salon of the Princesse Mathilde, surviving dynastic changes, extended into our own time. But these were exotic growths, anomalous to their generation. There have been imitations in later times; one is reminded of them to-day both in aristocratic quarters and amid the literary groups. The Lycée, where a good education is received at the public expense, is responsible for many changes in society. Women of no social position, by its means, obtain a unique prominence and power. But the historical salon, which was the instigator of original thought and the arbiter of taste and manners, was sacrificed by its own creation; it evoked a destroying spirit by whose agency, nevertheless, the position of women, as a whole, was incalculably raised. The salon came to an end with that society in which alone it could reach preëminence, and it can no more be rehabilitated than can the structure with which it fell.

It is difficult to realise the changes which have come over the daily life of women, and especially the life of the bourgeoisie, within the comparatively short time which has elapsed since the Revolution. The walks and drives, the multifarious shopping, the exchange of visits, the lectures, the concerts and plays, with which a woman may now fill her day, outside her four walls, were then unknown. It was not easy or safe to get about, the roads were dirty, uncomfortable, and even dangerous in Paris as in London. To conduct a salon it was obligatory for the hostess to be much at home, prepared to receive and to talk. The Princesse de Conti offered some form of entertainment every day ; the Duchesse de Choiseul, while her husband was in power, gave a supper nearly every evening ; the Princesse Mathilde seldom stirred from home ; and the salons, shrunken, changed, but still influential, of later years, were generally held by women who were incapacitated by delicate health from leaving their own firesides, and who were, therefore, always to be found ready for conversation. This was the case with the Comtesse d' Haussonville, the granddaughter of Madame de Staël and the wife and mother of Academicians, and also with the Marquise de Blacqueville ; both wrote, as did the beautiful and beloved Comtesse de Boulaincourt, who was an admirable talker, and whose varied gifts were much admired in the diplomatic circle. Mention of these salons of modern times would not be complete without the name of Madame Aubernon de Nerville, who belonged also to this later period.

V

It must be remembered that, before the Revolution, there were no journals to propagate ideas and spread the news, at least none worthy the name, for the timid government organs, such as the official gazettes, were instituted for the purpose of denying, rather than of revealing or disseminating the facts of the day, and the salon, assisted by the literary café, was the principal means by which opinion on current events was circulated.

But in the universal political awakening a curiosity before unknown sprang up in regard to the social systems of other lands. Frenchmen began to travel. Throughout the proud reign of Louis XIV, the French had never looked beyond their own borders, their own country containing, in their view, all that there was of civilisation. It was not until the eighteenth century that they awoke to the knowledge that there might be ideas worthy of attention elsewhere. England, by her form of government, had the greatest attraction for inquiring minds, whilst cultivated Englishmen flocked to Paris, drawn thither by the unparalleled society to be found in the brilliant salons. A social *rapprochement* between France and

England was the result, unique in the history of nations.

It was the heyday of Platonic friendship. Purely intellectual friendships between men and women, and their value, are seen, in the greatest degree, in the salons of the last half of the eighteenth century. To realise this one has only to examine the ties which existed between the Marquise Du Deffand and Horace Walpole, twenty years her junior ; between her friends the exquisite Duchesse de Choiseul and the wise Abbé Barthélemy; or, to pass to her rival, unhappy Julie de Lespinasse, do we not always think of her in juxtaposition with d' Alembert ? And Madame Geoffrin's devotion to the young King of Poland, which caused such a flutter throughout Europe in 1766 ; her friendship with Fontenelle who, on the other hand, was forty-two years her senior ; the connection—sentimental it is true—between Rousseau and Madame d' Houdetot ; these and others no less interesting emphasise the nature of the remarkable friendships which flourished in this period many of which added to the well-being, no less than to the mere enjoyment, of society.

It will be observed that these were, as a rule, friendships which were begun in maturity. Youth, the time of life when friendships are most easily and naturally formed, entered not at all into the scheme of intellectual eighteenth-century society which was marked by the absolute and undisputed reign of maturity and even age. The friendship which united Madame Du Deffand and Horace Walpole, Madame Geoffrin and Fontenelle, each begun when one was in middle life and the other old, was not an idiosyncrasy but was representative of the times.

The influence of women in France by the middle of the eighteenth century had become so powerful that a man could hardly rise without the co-operation of some one of them or, if he should succeed, he still remained obscure, unheeded ; and if, for instance, an Englishman living in Paris should attempt, as did Bolingbroke, to form a men's club, in imitation of those so popular in England,

it would have met with the same fate—
ignored by the women, and watched by the
authorities, it quickly died a natural death.

 In France, and in France alone in the
eighteenth century the men and women
followed the same pursuits and met continually. It was a natural result, therefore, that women should borrow mental
strength and independence from men, and
men gentleness and refinement from women.
"In each society," writes Saint Preux to
Julie,[1] "the mistress of the house is almost
always alone in the midst of a circle of men.
. . . . It is there that she learns to speak,
act, and think like them, and they like her."
Yet the idea that women should assume
any of the attributes of men was repugnant
to Rousseau and was contrary to his scheme
of society. He admitted, indeed, that
women were frivolous, deceitful, and inconstant :—

Speaking much but thinking little, feeling still less,
and wasting the best of themselves in vain chatter.

[1] *Julie ou la Nouvelle Héloïse*, J.-J. Rousseau, Paris: Garnier
Frères, p. 215.

But he added : All this appears to me to be their ex-
terior, like their paniers and rouge. These are showy
vices which it is necessary to have in Paris, and which
in reality cover sense, kindness, natural goodness.
They are less indiscreet, less busy-bodies than . . .
elsewhere. They are more solidly educated, and they
profit better from their instruction.

He could not therefore but admire women
who had attained intellectual eminence but
at the same time he feared that they were
going outside their proper sphere. "In a
word, if they displease me by all that characterises their sex which they have disfigured,
I esteem them by their conformity to ours
which does us honour ; and I find that they
would a hundred times rather be great men
than amiable women."[1]   Of this exceptional
condition of society, the salon of the later
eighteenth century was a representative product that could only have existed in Paris,
which, if it were the centre of the worst
follies, still remained the intellectual capital
of Europe, and a capital in which the intellectual quality constantly predominated.

[1] *Julie*, J.–J. Rousseau.   Paris : Garnier Frères, p. 222.

"When a man of weight introduces serious conversation . . . common attention is at once fixed on this new subject; men, women, the old, the young, all are ready to consider it in all its parts, and one is astonished at the sense and reason which is brought forth at will from all these giddy heads."[1] (And it was in this brilliant company that the mistress of a salon achieved her fame, impressing all those with whom she came in contact with her power.) "Everything," Rousseau remarks, apropos of the influence which women possessed in Paris, "depends on her; nothing is done but by her or for her; Olympus and Parnassus, glory and fortune, are equally under their laws. Books have a price, authors esteem, only so far as it pleases women to accord it."[2]

VI

Julie, wherein Rousseau thus describes the worth, the weaknesses, and the power

[1] *Julie*, J.-J. Rousseau. Paris : Garnier Frères, p. 296.
[2] *Ibid.*, p. 221.

of the Frenchwoman, appeared in 1760, when the salon was approaching the culminating point in its history. At this moment four particular salons were either fully developed or in process of formation, each of which represented a different stratum of society, and which, if not equally powerful, were each representative of an influential circle. Precedence among these must be given the salon of Madame Du Deffand. Socially and intellectually superior herself, her salon was distinguished by its select quality. The critical note in her *Lettres* indicates her intellectual fastidiousness, and in her salon the conversation was the wittiest, the brightest and lightest, and the society the most exclusive. Difficult to please, she inflexibly denied admittance to any who did not fulfil her exacting requirements. But from this very circumstance, in variety and in numbers, and so in the extent of her influence, Madame Geoffrin, who did not even pretend to know how to spell, excelled her.

The salon of Julie de Lespinasse rivalled both that of Madame Du Deffand and that

of Madame Geoffrin, containing the critical
and aristocratic features of the one and the
philosophical element for which the other
was celebrated, but in her own pre-emi-
nently feminine fashion Julie de Lespinasse undoubtedly stood alone.   Her
spontaneous and enthusiastic temperament, added to the genuine quality of her
character, made her beloved above any
other of those who aspired to a salon.
" Madame Geoffrin was feared ; Madame Du
Deffand admired; Madame Necker respected;
. . . Julie de Lespinasse loved."[1]   In the
field of the emotions lay her peculiar claim
to fame, and in this region of alternate storm
and sunshine she was without parallel.   As
in the case of Madame Du Deffand, it was
the posthumous publication of her letters
which brought Julie de Lespinasse into literary prominence, letters written, with the
exception of a few phrases which reflect the
influence of Rousseau, without affectation
and in the purest style.

[1] *Julie de Lespinasse*, par le Marquis de Ségur.   Paris : Calmann-
Lévy, p. 190.

Madame d' Épinay belonged by birth to the old noblesse, and her marriage to a bourgeois financier illustrates the modern rise and growth of wealth as a power in society. The combination of family and money in this marriage throws into relief the constructive phase amid the contradictory elements which were at work in France. She wrote on education, and her *Mémoires*, which are an invaluable key to the epoch, show her philosophical order of mind.

How then is it possible that Madame Geoffrin, of common origin, moderate means, and with no intellectual pretensions, should have aspired to and have obtained a place among the leaders of the most cultivated and intellectual society, and the most lavish in expenditure, that the world had to offer ? And not alone have gained a foothold but, in power and in influence, have surpassed them all ? For that this did happen is indisputably true.

In her native character in part, at least. may be found the answer. She was ambitious ; she possessed a strong will ; she

was persistent.   And she was blest with the
solid virtue of common sense.   It was her
predominant quality.   The success of Madame Geoffrin may also be laid to the times
in which she lived.   Louis XV was forced to
pay a heavy price for the withdrawal of the
court from Paris.   The King's absence, from
a monarchical point of view, had a disastrous
effect on his capital.   It laid the foundation
of its independence.   The court no longer
led the ideas and taste any more than it did
the fashion of the ancient city.   The court
met at Versailles, and Paris went its own
way, establishing, to the undoing of the court,
an alliance between its intelligence and its
wealth ; and it was now the genius of Paris,
its pride, its grace, its learning, its laughter,
which dominated Europe.[1]

It can easily be seen, therefore, that the
times were propitious for the furtherance of
personal ambition among the bourgeoisie.
In the previous century, Madame Geoffrin
could not have hoped to succeed in the plan

[1] *Portraits Intimes du Dix-Huitième Siècle*, E. and J. de Goncourt.   Paris: Bibliothèque-Charpentier, 1897, p. 137.

of life which, with consummate method, energy, and skill, she systematically followed throughout her long career ; she was now assisted by the forces of destiny itself.

VII

Great forces were indeed, as we now perceive, at work amid this brilliant society. The phrase Liberté, Égalité, Fraternité, born of the Revolution, has become so well known as almost, by popular repetition, to have lost its immense significance. Now the watchwords of a peaceful Republic, they are the negation of everything political in France before the Revolution, but at that very time the ideas on which these words are founded were put in practice in the salon.

From the inception of the salon perfect intellectual liberty, liberty of thought and liberty of discussion, was the very basis of the intercourse of which it was the centre, whether in the grand apartments of Madame de Rambouillet and Madame de Lambert or, later, in the modest rooms of Madame de Tencin and of Julie de Lespinasse.

The sense of fraternity, of good comradeship, of sympathy, was a paramount feature of the gatherings in the convent of Saint Joseph as in the rue Saint Honoré, though, as in every civilised society, be it small or great, rules of conduct were necessary, and rulers to enforce them. The mistress of a salon proved herself adequate both to formulate the laws which governed it and to undertake the duties of the lawgiver.

Equality of sex, of mind, and of person was never more conspicuous than in the salon of the eighteenth century. There the brilliant woman was listened to as attentively as the most erudite philosopher, and the words of Madame Du Deffand were as acceptable as the propositions of d'Alembert. Rank did not make a man welcome unless with it were combined engaging qualities of mind and manner and, thanks to common intellectual interests, the barriers of condition and of creed were, for the time, equally put aside.

In the salon, therefore, we find in active movement the ideas which were, when applied to existing political and social facts, to overthrow the old régime.)

MADAME DU DEFFAND

1697. Birth.

1718. Marriage.

1728. Separates from her husband.

1730. Enters into relations with President Hénault.

1739. Foundation of salon, rue de Beaune.

1747. Takes up her residence at the convent of Saint
Joseph, rue Saint Dominique. Salon enlarged.

1752. Threatened with blindness. Leaves Paris.
Meeting with Julie de Lespinasse.

1753. Returns to the convent of Saint Joseph, in Paris,
and reopens her salon.

1754. Is joined by Julie de Lespinasse.

1764. Rupture with Julie de Lespinasse and loss of
d'Alembert.

1765. Beginning of friendship with Horace Walpole.

1780. Death.

MADAME DU DEFFAND

I

IT is not always those who have taken the most active and prominent share in their time who are remembered by posterity, but persons who have had next to no influence on the current of events. The names of many of the leading politicians and writers of France in the eighteenth century are now seldom spoken, whilst some brilliant women who never wrote a book and never upset a minister appear to live with a vitality which has even a tendency to increase. It may be that this arises to some extent because they are types, and whether in history or in fiction it is the typical character that lives. And there is another thing to be said of Madame Du Deffand, who is undoubtedly such a woman as I have described—she offers such contrasts. There is a monotony of character about leading figures in the political or the literary world which drives the average reader to the novel-writer for refreshment ; but if he can find a man or a woman in real life who strikes by contrast with commonplace people, such a person at once gains something of the interest of the hero or heroine of the story ; and what arouses our curiosity and holds our attention in Madame Du Deffand is that contrast of character and life by which she is always startling us.

Madame Du Deffand is commonly remembered in England as the blind old friend of Horace Walpole, who was haunted by the absurd fear that the connexion of his name with that of a personage much more famous than himself—perhaps the most famous living woman—would bring down ridicule upon him, simply because she was old. When their friendship began, Walpole was, in the estimation of his contemporaries, a mere dilettante ; it was the publication of his correspondence after his death which gave his name the celebrity it now obtains. But by

Madame Du Deffand

From a painting. Artist unknown

(By permission of Messrs. Braun, Clement & Co.)

becoming more and more famous up to the time of her death, the picture of Madame Du Deffand, young, beautiful, and fascinating, is overshadowed by the more unusual figure of a woman, old, infirm, confined in a few small rooms in a convent, but attracting by the brightness of her mind every one, young and old, who came within her influence. It was in her youth, long before Walpole knew her, that Voltaire wrote:

> "Qui vous voit et qui vous entend
> Perd bientot sa philosophie;
> Et tout sage avec du Deffand
> Voudrait en fou passer sa vie."

A philosopher herself, her quarrel with the philosophers never ceased, nor did her friendship with their chief thinker.

In Madame Du Deffand's lifetime three kings successively occupied the throne of France, and the Duc d' Orléans, as Regent, in whose life she for a short time played a leading rôle, added to the demoralisation of society by his private life, notwithstanding his public virtues. She also may be said to have reigned by right of her intellectual and social pre-eminence, a rule which continued throughout the period of uncertainty and unrest which separated the old from the new order, when ancient faith and ways of thought were faltering before the impulse and rush of the new ideals with which the minds of Frenchmen were then filled.

In the early years of the eighteenth century, when the life of Louis XIV, and that era which the French call *le grand siècle*, with its wars, its glories, its tyrannies, and its taxations, was drawing to a close, and when dress, manners, art, and literature touched, and lingered for a brief moment at the summit of richness, elegance, and refinement—a fine, if decaying, fruit of civilisation—men still clung to the old social conditions. It was when the effect of the new ideas which attacked at once the State, the Church, and the family, was beginning to be felt, that Madame Du Deffand attained her majority and entered into this rapidly changing world.

Her portrait shows us a woman of clever and keen rather than beautiful aspect, but we are told so frequently by her contemporaries of her beauty, charm, and grace that we must abide by their decision. Her life, after the first reckless plunge into the fashionable and corrupt world about her, may be said to have been uneventful outwardly, and thenceforward she lived chiefly an intellectual existence, though she has left little besides her letters to mark it ; a short play, inimitable pen portraits, a few verses are all we have. These and her letters are sufficient, however, to show the precision of mind, the sure judgment, the exquisite literary taste, and the capacity which made men of the keenest intellect her admirers.

II

Marie de Vichy Champrond, afterward Marquise Du Deffand, was born in 1697, a year after the death of Madame de Sévigné, her great rival as a letter writer. The place of her birth is somewhat uncertain, but it is probable that it was the château de Champrond, Saône-et-Loire. Her parents

4

both belonged to noble families of Bourgogne. At six, according to usage, taken from the arms of her nurse, she was placed in a convent—that of Sainte Madeleine du Traisnel in Paris.

Madame Du Deffand early saw and combated every form of deceit; a passionate desire for truth was her dominant characteristic; it is seen in her references to her education, of which she often speaks bitterly as the cause of all the unhappiness of her life; she possessed, and made use of to a remarkable degree, that third eye of which Goethe speaks by which we are able to observe ourselves and our own actions as well as those of others, an unprejudiced and judicial eye which takes note of all that passes and weighs and judges. Such a mind is never satisfied with accepted truths, with dull routine or with petty details of commonplace living; contentment does not come readily to soaring spirits which, in a world where mediocrity obtains, flutter uselessly against the walls of environment, only to be hurt by aspiration. Independent and curious and enthusiastic, she wished to criticise, to examine, to know for herself.

So disturbing, even in childhood, were her questions on religion that Massillon was sent to argue with the precocious child in her convent. She trembled before the august presence of the renowned ecclesiastic, but not before his reasoning. Indeed the young pensionnaire sustained the discussion with so much sound sense that the future prelate left her more struck with her intelligence than scandalised by her heresies.

In the year 1718 she was married to the Marquis Du Deffand de la Lande. It was the usual *mariage de convenance* and was late for the wedding-day of so much wit and beauty, but her dot was small and the Marquis was undoubtedly the first suitor who was presented and, as he possessed the necessary qualifications, the marriage was concluded without delay. Unhappily, however, it united two persons dissimilar in character and temperament, a fact which was soon realised, especially by the young wife who quickly tired of her prosaic husband, and so they separated by amicable agreement. Once independent, Madame Du Deffand did not hesitate to enter upon the life of pleasure of the period; among the gayest of the fashionable world, beautiful and bright, she at once took a place among the reigning favourites. But she early emerged from some of the worst phases of society, and was soon cured of the passion for gambling, the scandal of the time. Years afterwards she wrote to Mr. Crawford, "I could, perhaps, procure you some amusements; but there is only one for you, which is your cursed play. Oh, what a detestable passion is play; I had it three months; it took me from everything. I thought of nothing else. Biribi was the game I loved. I was horrified at myself and I cured myself of that folly."[1] Gaming was indulged in to an even greater excess abroad than in England. In Paris the houses of private gentlemen were thrown

---

[1] *Correspondance complète de Madame Du D.* avec la duchesse de Choiseul, l'abbé Barthélemy et M. Crawfurt, publiée par M. le marquis de Sainte-Aulaire. Paris, 1877, t. i., p. 86.

open to the public, provided they played,
and at night the streets were lighted with
fire-pots before the houses of the grand
seigneurs which were converted into gaming establishments.   Even princesses of the
blood were not ashamed to profit by banks
established in their houses.

On Madame Du Deffand's entrance into
society her most intimate associates were of
a character ill calculated to the leading of a
reasonable life.   Her first friend was Madame
de Prie, wife of the French Ambassador
at Turin, whose life offers few redeeming
features, though she was not wanting in
esprit.   When Madame Du Deffand accompanied her to Normandy whither she
had been exiled, they characteristically began the day by exchanging verses before
getting up in the morning.   Madame de
Prie lived a dissolute life and, according
to the gossip of the time, died a wretched
death, though Madame Du Deffand declared
that she died simply from regret at no longer
possessing any political influence. Next
Madame de Parabère showed her the ways

of her unscrupulous world, introducing her
to the Regent's little suppers, which set the
fashion for this form of entertainment, con-
doling with her on her marriage, and regretting that she had not instead taken the vows
of a canoness.

In that case you would have been free; well placed
everywhere; with the status of a married woman; an
income which permits one to live and accept aid from
others; the independence of a widow, without the
ties which a family imposes; unquestioned rank,
which you would owe to no one; indulgence and
impunity. For these advantages there is only the
trouble of wearing a cross, which is becoming; black
or grey habits, which can be made as magnificent as
one likes; a little imperceptible veil, and a knitting
sheath.

Such tuition was not without its influence.
I will not attempt to give a detailed account of the manner of Madame Du Deffand's
life at this period, or relate her connexion
with Phillipe d'Orléans, and with his accomplished confidant in all manner of wild
dissipation, Delrieu Du Fargis, or her different experiences in the life of Paris of the
period. Abbé Galiani said that the women
of the eighteenth century loved with their

minds and not with their hearts, and it is always clear that Madame Du Deffand's heart was never in these enterprises but remained untouched until, in blind old age, a pale flower of love should bloom to be at once her expiation and her solace.

Long, however, before this singular event, Madame Du Deffand, unhappy, troubled, bored by her unsettled mode of life, made an effort to enter into closer relations with her husband. In 1728 a very curious letter was written in which are related the whole circumstances of this unsuccessful attempt at reconciliation. Monsieur Du Deffand was placed on probation ; he did not succeed in pleasing; overcome by the aversion and weariness, which the lady could not conceal, the unlucky husband did not linger, but at once saved the situation by taking his leave.

In her gay and uncontrolled youth we find Madame Du Deffand occasionally flitting from town to famous châteaux, of which many were reduced to ruins in the Revolution. We meet her bright face in the north with Madame de Prie at Courebévine, with

the Présidente de Berniére at La Rivière
Bourdet, and on the banks of the Loire in
old Touraine. She was one of the little
court at Sceaux gathered about the granddaughter of the great Condé, Louise de
Bourbon, the ambitious, intriguing brilliant
Duchesse du Maine, who did not a little to
retain for her the good graces of society.
For, after the second and final dismissal of
her husband, her friends pretended to be
shocked at what was called the lightness of
Madame Du Deffand's behaviour towards
him, though it was probable that it was
taste—the one unpardonable sin in Paris—
that was offended. But though Madame Du
Deffand in her youth paid little regard to
some of the rules which govern society, she
had good instincts and loved orderly conduct. Her youth was reckless rather from
the force of adverse circumstances than from
pure love of pleasure, and her intellect was
far too clear to allow her to continue in a
material and voluptuous existence. At
Sceaux, indeed, where the Duchesse du
Maine's passion for wit and brilliant con-

versation produced the saying that her guests were condemned to the "*galères du bel esprit,*" Madame Du Deffand was the one whose company was most desired. We read in the *Mémoires* of Madame de Staël, the humbly born, but clever companion of the Duchess this tribute to her talents :

No one has more wit or is more natural. The sparkling fire which animates her penetrates the inmost thought, draws it out, and throws into relief the faintest lines. She possesses to a supreme degree the talent of painting character, and her portraits, more living than the originals, make them better known than the most intimate connexion with them. She gave me an entirely new idea of this style of writing.[1]

A power of description in letters, the fashionable mental distraction of the early years of the century, and which had not yet lost vogue, was the one of her literary gifts by which Madame Du Deffand best pleased her contemporaries. She had a masculine order of mind, and all her writings are clear, terse, just, and sensible. She said that she did not know a rule of grammar, and

---

[1] *Nouvelle Collection des Mémoires*, Michaud et Poujoulat, Troisième Série, p. 758.

that she expressed herself by chance, independent of all method and all art, but in modern times Sainte-Beuve has ranked her letters as, next to Voltaire's works, the purest classics of the epoch, and d'Alembert rated her style with that of Madame de Sévigné. These remarkable women were alike in many ways—in wit, and in the irksomeness which everyday life had for them and, if the letters of Madame Du Deffand are wanting in the attractive spontaneity of those of Madame de Sévigné, they show a clearer insight into character. Madame de Sévigné's mind was objective, Madame Du Deffand's was subjective to the last degree.

It was Madame Du Deffand who urged the pleasure-loving abbés to their brightest sallies of wit, and she was the favourite whom Voltaire hoped to meet even when he had for companion the learned Marquise du Châtelet, his divine Émilie. Though among the company at Sceaux which included Madame de Lambert and the admirable Fontenelle, La Motte and d'Alembert, Madame Du Deffand was the acknowledged leader, those assembled there were, according to Voltaire and Malésieux, mere slaves of their hostess and though rules were relaxed for the *spirituelle* Marquise, whose presence was indispensable, and who had the choice of apartments and the day at her disposal still she, whose independent spirit chafed at the smallest restriction, must often have found these visits a trial. The death of the Duchess in 1753, however, freed her from the tax of this friendship.

The very contrasts of Madame Du Deffand's many-sided character were largely her charm : at once unaffected and artificial her life had been inconstant yet faithful ; ever feeling the need of friendship and companionship, no woman was more indifferent ; possessing little sentiment, she was not wanting in sensibility, and she sought in society a relief from the ennui which she declared was continual ; suspicious and confiding, in her own and other salons she could be in the same hour wise and frivolous, grave and gay. It was probably at Sceaux that this fascinating woman first met President Hénault, and began that intimacy which lasted while he lived, though she always had a rival, even after the lady's death, in Madame de Castelmoron. One of the most intellectual, gifted, and charming of this brilliant circle, writer, statesman, wit, and beau, President Hénault naturally appealed to a woman who was herself equally versatile. Between him and herself there already existed a tie through her aunt the Duchesse de Luynes, for whom Madame Du Deffand had a deep affection. On her side, the Duchess had given her sister's child from wayward youth much loving care and thought and the older woman's irreproachable life and assured position offered security to Madame Du Deffand who, though afraid neither of philosophers nor priests, stood in awe of this lofty character and substantial friend, whose reproaches alone she feared, and whose advice in affairs to which she attached importance she always asked. Her position in the Queen's household and the consideration shown her gave the Duchesse de Luynes many opportunities to forward the interests of

Charles Jean   François henault

Qui vive autant que son Ouvrage. *sp. de Cochin 1744*

Présenté par ses Neveux et Nièces

From an Engraving by Moitte after the Painting by St. Aubin.

her friends. President Hénault made her acquaintance in 1716 ; he pleased her, and it was she who introduced him to the Queen, Marie Leczinska. Through her good offices he was given the post of superintendent of the house, which procured for him, besides the five hundred thousand livres which appertained to the former occupant, an additional fifteen hundred francs. For Madame Du Deffand she obtained a pension of two thousand crowns from the Queen's treasury.

President Hénault did not forget what he owed the Duchess. "She has all the qualities of a most honest man ; noble, generous, faithful, discreet, enemy to all irony, proscribing slander which never approaches her house, considered by all the royal family, whom she sometimes receives,"[1] he wrote in his *Mémoires.*

After her second short and infelicitous trial of domestic life Madame Du Deffand lived with her brother, the treasurer of Sainte-Chapelle, until 1742, when she changed her

[1] *Mémoires du Président Hénault.* Paris, E. Dentu, 1855, p. 191.

quarters to the rue de Beaune, taking rooms in the small house where Voltaire subsequently died. Here the first representatives of the world of fashion and letters were to be found and the brilliant company soon began to be talked about.

But it is the modest apartment in the convent of Saint - Joseph, first occupied by Madame Du Deffand in 1747, which is known as her salon. Founded by Madame de Montespan, this religious house is now merged into the War Office of the Republic; but if one turns off the old aristocratic boulevard Saint-Germain and strolls down the rue Saint-Dominique, its yellow walls and sunny court may still be seen. The graceful spires of Sainte-Clotilde have since sprung high aloft across the place before its grated windows, and the old bridges that span the Seine have been cleared of the picturesque four-story buildings that then encumbered them; but the Palais Bourbon, now the Chamber of Deputies, whose erection Madame Du Deffand must have witnessed, is just around the corner; it was the heart of the fashionable quarter of Paris. Long before she entered it, the convent had received many well-known persons within its shelter, beginning with the celebrated protectress herself. The Pretender lived here in hiding three years under the most extraordinary and romantic conditions, smuggled mysteriously from chamber to chamber, assisting, unsuspected, at conversations where his own fortunes were sometimes the principal topic. Here Madame Du Deffand lived twenty-seven years—until her death, October 24, 1780. For ten years Julie de Lespinasse was her companion, and Madame de Genlis was also an occupant of the convent at this time. Madame Du Deffand had the apartment formerly belonging to Madame de Montespan, whose arms may still be seen above the mantelpiece. She gave to its furnishing much thought and taste, and the fame of her Monday night suppers, where the best conversation in Paris was to be found, extended across the channel. From this time her salon was the meeting place for all celebrities, French or foreign. But she would have nothing to do with politics any more than with philosophy though all parties and varied principles were represented by their most able advocates ; neither should her salon be termed literary, for the fashionable and frivolous were made as welcome as the learned, if only they had wit and manners.

The literary ability of the women of the salons cannot be measured by their writings. Authorship for women was not fashionable, and they were careful to disclaim any pretension to it. Their *métier*—and Madame Du Deffand was supreme in this—was to rule. They, themselves, posed as ignorant, and any compositions which have come down to us were written only for private perusal; sparkling bon-mots, glancing epigrams, witty verses, meant social success and distinction. It was an airy, daring flight of light comedy that the age exacted.

III

Madame Du Deffand was now fifty years

old, and her life on entering the convent
was supposed to be reformed, though she
said she would not do rouge and the
President the honour of giving them up.
Her existing friendships, with the exception of d'Alembert, were thenceforward
to be unbroken. Every day, beside Hénault, she saw Pont de Veyle, her loyal
friend from childhood, a nephew of the
talented, conspiring Madame de Tencin, a
friend also of Maurepas, whose disgrace he
shared. A writer of clever comedies, stories, and verses, but silent, morose, un-
pleasing, it was, according to Walpole, the
art of parody, which he possessed to an
extraordinary degree, that made Pont de
Veyle popular and that changed his whole
appearance when he astonished the company by his exhibitions of wit and satire.
There was Formont, too, who, until Voltaire's intimacy with Madame Du Châtelet
began, was his closest friend; this new
phase in Voltaire's life also caused a break
in his correspondence with Madame Du
Deffand and when, fourteen years later,

5

at Madame Du Châtelet's death, it began anew, the former tone of intimacy was lost.

In the meantime Formont had taken a foremost place with Madame Du Deffand, and at his death, in 1758, she begged Voltaire to perpetuate the memory of his old friend in writing ; but he received the news somewhat coldly and her hope of immortality for Formont's name in Voltaire's pages was disappointed. A devoted friend, a charming companion, clever, without pedantry, above conceit, Formont was one of the most beloved and agreeable in this company where the gentler virtues must sometimes have been missed. He had his prototypes among Englishmen in Storer, Hare, and Crawford, who were of the same period ; amiable, lovable, and with numberless friends each wasted much of life on play and in fashionable follies ; clever and able, each led a somewhat useless existence, leaving behind him but little trace of the capacity and brilliant gifts which he possessed. The Chevalier d' Aydie, the lover

VOLTAIRE.

After the Drawing at Ferney.

of Mademoiselle Aïssé[1] was also one of the
constant frequenters of Madame Du Deffand's salon when he was in Paris, and it
was here that he met the beautiful Circas-
sian who remains a touching and romantic
figure in an epoch when it was a misfortune
to possess deep feeling. Monsieur de Ferriol, the French Minister to Constantinople
in the early part of the century, brought a
beautiful child who had been exposed for
sale in the slave market, to Paris, and had
her educated as his daughter. The attempt
to reconcile the ideals of an elevated nature
with the corrupt society of the period was
beyond her strength and she died early, the
victim of an unhappy passion.

It is odd that, of the three men who
directed French ideas to reform, and finally
inflamed to revolution, two should be lifelong friends and correspondents of Madame
Du Deffand, to whom such opinions were
so unsympathetic. Of Rousseau, her opinion was unfavourable to the point of dislike

[1] Mademoiselle Aïssé, 1695–1733, left an interesting correspondence.

and hostility, though one would gather
from Walpole that she did not notice him :

> She never interested herself about Rousseau nor
> admired him. Her understanding is too just not to
> be disgusted with his paradoxes and affectations; and
> his eloquence could not captivate her, for she hates
> eloquence. She asked no style but Voltaire's, and
> has an aversion to all moral philosophers. She has
> scarce mentioned Rousseau living or dead ; and
> d'Alembert was egregiously mistaken in thinking she
> wrote my letter to him ; Rousseau would have been
> still more offended had he known how little she ever
> thought on him. She was born and had lived in the
> age of true taste and had allowed no one but Voltaire
> to belong to it. She holds that all the rest have cor-
> rupted their taste and language. La Fontaine is her
> idol ; that is, simplicity is.[1]

For Rousseau she had the contempt
and scorn which she felt for the philosophers in general and for their work, whose
destructive tendency she was one of the
few to understand. She seemed, at times,
indeed, to see into the future, often in
her letters uneasily alluding to the common people, already reading in their discontent something to be feared although, more
happy than her friend, the Duchesse de

[1] *Letters of Horace Walpole*, ed. Toynbee, vol. x., p. 289.

Choiseul, she did not witness the final reckoning. Montesquieu, like Voltaire, found inspiration in her society, and so she contributed all unwittingly to his greatest work, which she is said to have noticed only by the famous bon-mot "qu'il n'y avait dans *l'Esprit des Lois* de Montesquieu que de l'esprit sur les lois." When, however, the author was criticised as having made egotism the foundation of all actions and the lever which moved society she cynically remarked "Good, he has only revealed every one's secret." Their correspondence is full of wit and humour and of eighteenth-century vivacity and freedom of expression, bringing before one the aërial, graceful, artificial posturing of Fragonard, the quaint, ugly, delightful figures of Watteau.

When she writes that she is blind he thus seeks to console her : "Do you not see that we were formerly, you and I, little rebel spirits who were condemned to the shades ? It ought to console us that those who see clearly do not on that account give out light." Voltaire, who had made verses be-

fore to her *beaux yeux*, with characteristic
vanity seized the opportunity to display his
skill in turning rhymes, rather than to express
any real emotion :

"Oui, je perds les deux yeux; vous les avez perdus
O sage Du Deffand.   Est-ce une grande perte ?
Du moins nous ne reverrons plus
Les sots dont la terre est couverte.
Et puis tout est aveugle en cet humain séjour;
On ne va qu'à tâtons sur la terre et sur l'onde;
On a les yeux bouchés à la ville, à la cour;
Plutos, la Fortune et l'Amour
Sont trois aveugle-nés qui gouvernent le monde."

The death, in 1750, of the Marquis Du
Deffand, whom his wife probably had not
seen since the ineffectual attempt at reconciliation of which I have already spoken, she
seemed, nevertheless to feel.   The terror of
oncoming blindness threatened to make existence a blank.   She could not bear solitude,
yet society for the moment was insupportable, and to the surprise and dismay of her
friends she announced her determination to
leave Paris for ever.   But the tranquillity
and repose which she sought were not to
be found either at the château de Champrond

with her brother, or at Lyons, where she had been attracted by her friendship for the Cardinal de Tencin. One thing was impossible for this remarkable woman—she could not become a provincial, and she made known her intention of returning to Paris in the following year.

It was at the château de Champrond that there commenced a famous connexion which filled a large place for many years in Madame Du Deffand's life ; for it was here she met Julie de Lespinasse,[1] whose position in the household as an unrecognised relative, dependent and solitary, was far from happy. Madame Du Deffand soon perceived this and, captivated by her self-reliant character and her accomplishments, presently formed the idea of attaching the clever and agreeable young woman to herself as a resource in failing sight. The following letter written to her while negotiations with the family were proceeding would, ten years later, have read as if Madame Du Deffand had received

---

[1] Julie de Lespinasse was the natural daughter of Madame Du Deffand's brother, the Comte de Vichy and the Comtesse d'Albon.

some warning of the blow to her pride and affection which was to fall upon her through this engaging girl in the division of her salon and in the loss of d'Alembert, her most cherished friend :

If you knew me well, you would have no anxiety over the way in which I shall treat your self-esteem; the least artifice and the least little art in your conduct would be insupportable to me. I am naturally distrustful and all those in whom I discern artfulness become suspicious to me to the point of being no longer able to have any confidence in them. I have two friends, Formont and d'Alembert. I love them passionately, not so much for their personal attractiveness and for their friendship for me as for their extreme truthfulness. You must then resolve to live with me in the greatest frankness and sincerity, never to employ either insinuation or exaggeration; in a word, never to lose one of the greatest attractions of youth, which is candour. You have a good deal of intelligence, you have gaiety, you are capable of sentiment; with all these qualities you will be charming as long as you remain without pretension and without deceit.[1]

Julie thankfully accepted Madame Du Deffand's proposal, and promised to abide

[1] *Correspondance complète de Madame Du Deffand,* ed. de M. de Lescure, Paris, 1865, t. i., p. 195.

by her conditions. The history of their connexion for ten years and its sudden end, the defection of d'Alembert and the rival salon set up by the younger woman, is an oft-told tale. Madame Du Deffand was fifty-seven, Julie de Lespinasse twenty-two, when their lives approached so closely. Afflicted with sleeplessness, Madame Du Deffand only arose in time to receive at six. Her intelligent companion, thus left her freedom, was in readiness earlier, and there and then made the havoc among the guests which had such wide results and which was the beginning of her own salon. It was d'Alembert, the "petit ami," whose advent and progress in the social and literary world Madame Du Deffand had so zealously assisted and jealously guarded, who helped Julie in this double rôle, and who led the choicest spirits among the Marquise's following to her rival ; Turgot, Condorcet, and Marmontel were among the number who were wont to assemble in Julie's own apartment. Naturally as soon as Madame Du Deffand became aware of this breach of faith all harmony was at an end between the two women. The philosophical coterie which Julie de Lespinasse then joined wrote much on this personal and rather trivial subject, and generally to the discredit of Madame Du Deffand, whom they accused of harshness and jealousy, but, as they never forgave her for not uniting with them, their justice is to be suspected. As for Julie, she was charged with inconstancy, strong passions, and deceit. She had the good taste, however, to allude to Madame Du Deffand, after their estrangement in terms of respect and gratitude.

This experience embittered the remainder of Madame Du Deffand's life, for with the exception of Walpole, she never wholly trusted any one again. Old and blind, she who gave and demanded exclusive affection now perceived her oldest friends divide their allegiance between her and the woman she had driven from her, and herself forsaken quite by d'Alembert, who had been a daily visitor for twenty years. She struggled hard to retain him. How changed the proud-spirited Marquise! Humble, patient, and long suffering under his rude rebuffs, she yet endeavoured to preserve some part of their old friendship.

To a letter from Germany in which he wrote that he would not trouble her for an answer but that he hoped to receive news of her through Julie—with whom he was in constant communication—she replied at once:

No! No! Monsieur, no one shall take my place to give you news of me and still less to reply to the the most charming letter which I have received from you. In reading it, I thought I was twenty years younger, than I was at Sainte-Chapelle, that you were as much pleased with me as I was with you. Finally this letter recalled the golden age of our friendship ; it reawakened my tenderness ; it made me happy. Let us start from there, believe me, and let us love one another as much as we have done. I believe that we could not do better ; believe it also if you are able. . . . Adieu my dear d' Alembert ; I am and shall always be the same to you. Do not doubt it, and love me in your turn.[1]

This touching appeal brought no response. It was the last letter she ever wrote to him.

[1] *Julie de Lespinasse*, par le Marquise de Ségur.   Paris: Calmann Lévy, p. 141.

But his was the sole instance of the entire loss of an old friend. Several of the habitués, however, without giving up their places in Madame Du Deffand's circle, were also frequenters of the salon of her protégée and rival. It was even rumoured that President Hénault himself proposed marriage to Julie. Madame Du Deffand never forgave her and seldom spoke her name. Her only comment to Walpole in repeating the news of her death, in 1776, was: "She should have died sixteen years earlier, I should not have lost d'Alembert." "If she is in Paradise," she wrote to another friend, "the Holy Virgin had better take care, for she may rob her of the affection of the Eternal Father."

But the vacant place in her heart was— strangely enough—to be taken by an Englishman. Julie de Lespinasse opened her salon in 1764; the next year Horace Walpole, visiting the Continent, was introduced to Madame Du Deffand, for no foreigner of distinction now passed through Paris without, if he wished to know its society, seeking admission there. Her appearance at

this time of her life was singularly attractive. She was quite blind, but there was
nothing disfiguring or distressing to an observer in this affliction ; her eyes were
closed, but too proud to wish to be pitied
she endeavoured to conceal her loss of sight
as far as possible ; her features retained their
regularity and delicacy, and her complexion
its freshness. The quaint simplicity of her
dress, which never varied, added to the
charm which seemed to envelop her. Her
face was framed within frills of lace, and a
knot of ribbon beneath the chin fastened a
black velvet hood ; she wore a jacket, also
of black velvet, which opened over a white
dress trimmed with deep ruffles of lace. In
her letters she complains of her serious
and melancholy disposition, but those who
knew her, on the contrary, have left an impression of her liveliness and gaiety, and
they tell us that, above all, she fascinated
by her conversation, and never more so
than at this time of her life when she had
long left youth behind, and when before
her was the prospect of an infirm and love-

less old age. It was with this celebrated woman, now sixty-eight years old, whose life had been so full, so vivid, and so varied, that Walpole, who was twenty years younger, began an intimacy which has become historical, and has linked together forever two personalities differing both in nationality and character. Walpole wrote cynically on friendship, but he did not put his superficial theories into practice; while Madame Du Deffand argued that it were better to be dead than not to love someone, he maintained that it were better to be dead than to love any one; the old dispute of pain or gain, sung by Oriental, by latter-day poets, was gone over again between them. Though Walpole exacted a promise that his letters should be destroyed, he carefully hoarded those he received from her and in them we find more incomparable portraits and hear many keen reflections on the people and events of the period. Her correspondence, which extended over a period of forty-one years, ends two days before her death with a letter to him on whom her thoughts were fixed, and to whom had been given the tenderest feelings of her heart. "I have not the strength to be frightened," she wrote, in reference to her state, "and never expecting to see you again, I have nothing to regret."[1]

In spite of her pessimistic views concerning the regard in which she was held by her friends, Madame Du Deffand was surrounded by them to the last moment of her life. The Duchesse de Choiseul and the Maréchales de Luxembourg and de Mirepoix hardly left her bedside in her last illness. Still she could not believe that their devotion was inspired by affection and, surprising Wiart, her faithful secretary, in tears, she whispered, "Do you love me then?" They were her last words.

IV

The Parisian society of the eighteenth century is little understood. There were in it so many different shades; the *Mémoires* of Madame d'Épinay show but

---

[1] *Correspondance complète de Madame Du Deffand*, ed. de M. de Sainte-Aulaire, t. i., p. cxxxii.

one phase, as do those of other letter-writers; the salon of Madame Geoffrin was another world, for in spite of her royal intimacies she remained to the end of her days a *bourgeoise*, and her salon distinctly indicated the influence of her ordinary origin; she never had the entrée to that select society which exemplified the ancient noblesse, and which still held to the old traditions and pretended to an elegance above academical, clerical, philosophical, or court coteries. At Madame Geoffrin's death, the imposing ceremonies, the funeral orations, drew from Madame Du Deffand the caustic criticism "Voila bien du bruit pour une omelette au lard."[1] It is probable, also, that she had not forgotten the sting of Madame Geoffrin's unprecedented act of hospitality and homage towards Julie de Lespinasse when, on her departure from Saint-Joseph, she was asked, the only woman, to Madame Geoffrin's favoured Wednesdays, the day set apart for men of

[1] *Correspondance complète de Madame Du Deffand*, ed. de M. de Sainte-Aulaire t. i , p. xcii.

letters, and more exclusive, if less lively, than the Mondays.

The salon of Madame Du Deffand was not easy of access as has been seen in the case of Rousseau. Genius alone was not a passport to her favour. It was imperative that her standard be reached in every particular, and elegant manners, gaiety, and good sense were necessary qualifications. Of Marmontel she said: "How much trouble he takes, how he exerts himself to be witty. He is only a vagabond clothed in rags!"[1] Neither was she complimentary to Diderot, who never crossed the threshold but once. "Nous n'avons pas d'atomes crochus,"[1] she said. Grimm she never would receive at all. The Maréchales de Luxembourg and Mirepoix, the Duchesse de la Vallière, the Duc and Duchesse de Choiseul, the Prince and Princesse de Beauvau, the Boufflers,— all the most considered in society, gathered about her chair, the famous tonneau of which we hear frequent mention

[1] *Correspondance complète de Madame Du Deffand,* ed. de M. de Sainte-Aulaire t. i., p. xcii.

6

in her letters. The latest ideas were discussed; statesmen and a few favoured philosophers, poets, pretty and clever women,
and men of the world who were agreeable
and cultivated only, displayed their wit,
charm, or beauty, and proved their right to
be there; she never allowed the conversation
to become either dull or vapid; it was intellectual, but not heavy, and the agitating
questions discussed by the encyclopédists
were brought up only as subjects of ridicule.
Sometimes, tired of French vivacity, she
would turn to Madame Necker, the fair, blue-
eyed provincial Swiss, and would spend an
evening with her at Saint-Ouen.

The salon of the eighteenth century, historical though it has become, is, to the foreign mind, apt to convey the idea of crowded
receptions and grand apartments. The word
seems to eliminate the life, and causes us
to forget that we must understand by it the
complete environment of some celebrated
and remarkable persons—the reception of
the savant and the politician, the confidences
of the dearest friends. As we know, Madame

Du Deffand received her guests in a small parlour, and in this unpretentious interior the social salon, the highest form of agreeable and intellectual society that the world has ever seen, attained its most complete development. I have said that, of Madame Du Deffand's contemporaries, Madame Geoffrin belonged to a less exclusive society, of which the philosophers were the leading spirits ; Julie de Lespinasse and Madame d' Épinay were also supporters of the philosophical party to which, in spite of her intimate friendships with their chiefs, Madame du Deffand was distinctly inimical; of this unique group of women, Madame d' Épinay alone survived Madame Du Deffand, whose salon was a survival more nearly resembling the seventeenth- than the eighteenth-century product. The influence of the philosophical salons, the freedom with which political and philosophical topics were generally argued, assisted materially in the overthrow of the ancient society of which she was a perfect and a final example and the burning fever of politics, to culminate a few years later in revolution, soon overthrew completely the reign of fashion, of taste, of caste, of theories.

V

It was not easy for an Englishman to gain a reputation for esprit among the quickest intellects of France, but it was in this exclusive coterie that the figure of Horace Walpole suddenly emerged. He was well received at Court and was shown marked attention by the Queen, whose presence he left with an apt quotation from his favourite Madame de Sévigné : *La reine est le plus grand roi du monde*. He was made welcome everywhere, for he became the fashion; his amusing conversation, which his bad French only accentuated, and his manner of jesting—for the letter to Rousseau, pretending to come from Frederic of Prussia, ill-natured and unkind though it seemed to the friends of the susceptible and sensitive philosopher—set all Paris laughing and made him the most talked-of man about town. Though he professed to be satiated with society, he prolonged his stay in Paris and confessed to some concern at leaving. "I almost regret having come here," he wrote home, "I love the manner of living and have become attached to so many persons as to make me feel more regret in leaving than I would have believed."

Whether we regard his friendship with Madame Du Deffand as an incident in her life or as a phase in the social life of France and England in the eighteenth century how noteworthy it is, illustrating as it does the singular attraction of each of these friends. Glance back over Madame Du Deffand's life, her youth, her marriage, her attachments, her experiences, and at last her affection centred on Walpole, a foreigner, imitative only of the French spirit. She had passed the age of gallantry, a period which was as fixed in public opinion before the Revolution as the coming and going of day and night; she could, therefore, in her opinion—which therein differed from Walpole's —give herself freely to the fond attachment, the mental exhilaration, which his original personality and mind inspired in her. Wal-

pole remained in Paris seven months, and
on the day of his return began their correspondence, which continued fourteen years,
—to the end of her life. At first he went to
see her out of curiosity; then, always interested in the private life of great personages,
to hear about the Regent and the gay society of her youth that laughed, danced, and
coquetted at the Palais-Royal and Saint-
Cloud. From these first interviews he went
away saying—rather rudely and untruth-
fully, if he himself is to be believed—that
he had to listen to a great deal of dull talk
on what was going on at the time in order
to extract from her some details of the life
of the Regent. But a few weeks disclosed a
marked change in his sentiments, and created
a memorable friendship. It was very human,
originating in exchanges of congenial wit
and shrewdness ; it certainly on his part,
too, rose to affection. '' My dear old friend ''
were the words in which he constantly
spoke of her after her death ; simple enough
in themselves, their very spontaneity and
unaffectedness in the middle of phrases be-

came unmistakable marks of their truth, and revealed some depth of feeling. So far as his sensitiveness to opinion would permit— for her advanced years, which appeared to her a safeguard against comment, to him seemed to furnish a handle for ridicule, the fear of which was always uppermost in his mind—his deference and tenderness toward her were unfailing. Walpole visited Paris at different periods, and from their first meeting he found a place in the still passionate heart hitherto never really touched. She had Wiart, her faithful secretary, taught English that Walpole might be spared the trouble of writing in a foreign tongue; when he was ill she begged him to send a daily bulletin of his health.

Attached though he undoubtedly was to her, Walpole, as has been said, was a little ashamed of the devotion he inspired, and often unreasonably and unkindly reproved her for what he considered its too open and frequent expression. What pathetic and touching words, what an unusual exhibition of feeling, from a woman of seventy are here disclosed!

I thought one day that I was a garden of which you were the gardener; that seeing winter arrive, you uprooted all the flowers which you did not judge to belong to the season, although there were still some which were not entirely faded, like little violets, little marguerites, . . . and that you had left but one certain flower which has neither odour nor colour, which one calls the immortelle, because it never fades. . . . It is the emblem of my soul in which is a great privation of thought but where a great constancy, esteem, and attachment remains.[1]

But, devoted though she was to him, Madame Du Deffand was never long deceived in any one, and her keen instincts and sound judgment pierced through the egotism which others saw, to find Walpole's true weakness in that fear of ridicule from which she herself was to suffer continually. Walpole's character has been described over and over again, but his besetting sin has never been more cleverly handled than in her portrait of him :

You have a weakness which is unpardonable, you sacrifice your feelings to it, your conduct is guided by it; it is the fear of ridicule. It makes you dependent on the opinion of fools, and your friends are not safe from the impressions which fools may wish to give

[1] *Correspondance de Madame Du Deffand*, ed. de M. de Sainte-Aulaire, t. i., p. ci.

you against them.   Your mind is easily disturbed.   It
is a drawback of which you are aware and which you
may remedy by the firmness with which you follow
your resolutions.[1]

There are many proofs that Walpole's attachment to Madame Du Deffand was genuine, and fragments of letters show him to
possess not only the keen perception which
has been universally accorded him, but that
for which he has less often been given credit
—a good heart. It may be that he was
drawn at first toward Madame Du Deffand
by the intellectual resemblance she bore to
Madame de Sévigné:

I have heard her dispute with all sorts of people,
on all sorts of subjects, and never knew her in the
wrong.   She humbles the learned, sets right their
disciples, and finds conversation for everybody.   Affectionate as Madame de Sévigné, she has none of her
prejudices, but a more universal taste; and with the
most delicate frame, her spirits hurry her through a life
of fatigue that would kill me were I to continue here.[2]

It has been claimed for Walpole himself
that his letters compare with those of Ma-

---

[1] *Correspondance de Madame Du Deffand,* ed. de M. de Sainte-
Aulaire, t. i., p. xcix.
[2] *Letters of Horace Walpole,* ed. Toynbee, vol. vii., p. 315.

dame de Sévigné, but his crowd of notes,
the anecdotes hoarded and rewritten, prove
how far he was from her unstudied simplicity, though he took her for his model.
His letters are less literary in form, less
elevated in tone, and they show him to be
more of a gossip—it is not, perhaps, their
least claim to our gratitude—than either of
the women whose correspondence he held
so high. His haunting fear of ridicule,
though not heroic, is perhaps not, after
all, unnatural in this connexion — given
a supersensitive, hypercritical man of forty-
seven and a blind woman of seventy—and
the order for the destruction of his letters
from a man who was regarding them from
the point of view of literary material may be
charitably urged as a matter of discretion.
Madame Du Deffand's correspondence, already famous, was valuable, and he knew it
would be likely some day to be published.
Besides, towards the end of the reign of
Louis XV all letters coming from England
were opened in Paris, and were likely to be
sent to Versailles if they contained the names

HORACE WALPOLE.
From a Painting by N. Hone.

of well-known people or anything amusing to the Court. His precautions, therefore, seemed to him proper as a prudent measure of self-protection.

It is difficult for the foreigner to understand the English character, but Madame Du Deffand was always quick to note the underlying principles which govern action.

You English submit to no rule, to no method [she wrote]. You would have all the intelligence that you have even though no one had any before you. Ah! we are not like that! We have books on the art of thinking, of writing, of comparing, of judging! We are the children of art.[1]

The keen French woman had seized upon the true character of the English mind, which seldom reasons from any general proposition; the Englishman says what comes into his head, often regardless of any thought for proportion, grace, or ulterior fitness, because he belongs so largely to a race in which the art instinct is not developed. But this absence of feeling and of respect for art is conducive to a candour,

[1] *Correspondance de Madame Du Deffand*, ed. de M. de Sainte-Aulaire, t. i., p. xciv.

a freshness, and an individuality of thought and action, which are as foreign to the other, and which that other finds original and admirable.

Another Englishman, young, charming, and witty, had been earlier taken within Madame Du Deffand's intimate circle. This was James Crawford, of Renfrewshire, a well-known figure in London society who was playfully called the "Fish" by his English contemporaries. It was he who introduced Walpole to the convent of Saint Joseph and thus attached Madame Du Deffand to him by the added tie of gratitude. Her acquaintance with Hume, whose sobriquet of the "paysan de la Danube" was obtained in her salon—and who, by the way, left a legacy to d'Alembert—was also due to Crawford:

You hold me fast by two strong chords [she wrote Crawford, in 1773], inclination and gratitude. I do not need to tell you on what the inclination is founded. You are not ignorant that you are very amiable, and that your small defects are effaced by an infinite number of excellent qualities . . . and then just now the souvenir of Mr. Hume, without counting the glory, gives me much pleasure; I am writing to him incessantly." [1]

Nevertheless, Hume and his ideas were outside her sympathies, and she did not care for his set—which included Julie de Lespinasse—in Paris. For Crawford she had a deep and tender affection, and their exchange of letters is another valuable addition to literature. Like those to Walpole, they are personal and intimate in tone, and show her passionate wish for exclusive affection. Crawford might well have been styled an *ennuyé*, and Madame Du Deffand could and did sympathise with this bent of mind: "You who have the misfortune as well as I to be always bored!"[2] she writes. Their correspondence was begun after he had introduced Walpole to the convent of Saint-Joseph, and was continued by her perhaps in the hope of keeping in closer touch with Walpole as well as by regard for Crawford; but the melancholy, which was the found-

[1] *Correspondance complète de Madame Du Deffand*, ed. de M. de Sainte-Aulaire, t. i., p. 32.

[2] *Ibid.*, i., p. 25.

ation of his character, attracted her, as did
the amiable qualities and quick wit which
made him so well liked in Parisian society.

"Little Crawford is a very unhappy being," she wrote to Walpole. "He has bad
health, but his mind is worse. I do not
know what will become of him; nothing
could be like his uncertainty; ennui is con-
suming him, I pity him."[1]

Belonging to a younger generation than
Walpole, Crawford was one of that fashionable and clever group in London, of whom
Charles James Fox was the leader, and
the Fifth Earl of Carlisle a striking figure,
the group of young men which, with
Fitzpatrick, the "beau Richard," Anthony
Storer, the "Bon Ton," and Hare, of many
friends, George Selwyn, though of opposite
politics to some of them, patronised and
made much of. These young men, outside
their social, literary, and artistic tastes, were
possessed of political ambition; they stood
by each other in the elections and in office;

[1] *Correspondance complète de Madame Du Deffand*, ed. de
M. de Sainte-Aulaire, t. i., p. cii.

they made verses, flirted, set the fash-
ions, and enjoyed in each other's society
the flashes of wit, epigrammatic sayings,
and *bon mots* which delighted their world.
Crawford, as well as Walpole, has suffered
from the criticism of posterity; perhaps his
character has not been given justice. He
was probably better appreciated abroad,
where he spent the greater part of his life,
than at home, where he was possibly not so
well understood, and where he was accused
of insincerity, affectation, and jealousy.
At any rate he was beloved in France.
Dutens devoted some pages to him in his
Mémoires, in which he is described under
the name of Astaque:

Astaque is the most singular compound in nature:
the versatility of a mind full of original and capricious
ideas; his warm heart, his quick blood, his spleen,
his vivacious spirit, his feeble body, all that forms
separately one individual which would suffice to com-
pose half a dozen distinctly marked characters, and
which together presents the most extraordinary being
that one could meet in society. . . . Astaque has an
elevated mind; the birth and wealth of those with
whom he associates do not affect him in the least; he
finds that he has enough both of one and the other to

be on a level with any. Add that Astaque is good, charitable, humane, quick-tempered, and gentle, a warm friend, a generous enemy (if it can be that he has enemies); impatient by temperament, indulgent by reflection, naif one moment and in another full of sallies of wit, enjoying little, often bored, making delicious projects to amuse himself, putting none into execution; he has spoken of it, it is enough.[1]

The English may be, in some cases, criticised for their lack of hospitality towards the refugees hurried to their shores by the Revolution, many of whom had lavished hospitality upon their countrymen in Paris, but Crawford cannot be charged with ingratitude. Letters, still extant, from Talleyrand, the Comte de Verdreuil, the Comte de Pomblanc, and others, prove the sterling character of the regard which made him hasten to the assistance of those of the old coterie whom he met again under such trying circumstances. His death in London, in 1814, again called forth warmest expressions of attachment from Paris. Walpole and Crawford, separated by disparity in years, if not in character, would not nat-

[1] Cited in *Correspondance complète de Madame Du Deffand*, ed. de M. de Sainte-Aulaire, t. iii., p. 388.

urally have been intimate, but Madame Du Deffand attempted to draw these two together; for would not unanimity in friendships form another link to bind Walpole to her?

But the prolonged visits of Walpole and Crawford were not isolated cases of social *rapprochement* between the two countries in that age of friendships. George Selwyn was the representative figure of these international relations in England, Madame Du Deffand in France. The connection between English and French high society was closer at this period than before or since in its history. To be sure the attractions of Paris seemed to be greater to the Englishman than those of London to the Frenchman, but if, then as now, the latter, attached in a greater degree to his own environment, less seldom left home, England attracted him socially and politically and was the land of his choice when he was led by inclination or necessity to travel.

At this period, when the French salons and hôtels of the boulevard Saint-Germain

7

were in their glory, Englishmen of wit and fashion constantly lived in Paris for long periods. During Burke's visit, in 1773, he was often present at Madame Du Deffand's supper parties, and even Wilkes might have been found there. In 1751 Lord Bath writes home of an evening at Madame Du Deffand's: "When the conversation fell upon England, they knew," he wrote, "its history better than we ourselves."[1] In one of her letters to Crawford —letters in general so demonstrative that Walpole's conceit might have been touched and his uneasiness have considerably abated had he had access to them—Madame Du Deffand translates verses Charles James Fox addressed to Mrs. Crewe, and tells of her pleasure on again seeing the great Parliamentary leader.

I was charmed to see him again, I had his name repeated four or five times when he was announced, unable to believe that it was he; I thought him in the midst of Parliament at the head of the Americans. M. de Beuvau entered a moment after his arrival; I

[1] *Correspondance complète de Madame Du Deffand*, ed. de M. de Sainte-Aulaire, t. i., p. lxv.

asked if he knew him, he said he did not. "Eh,
bien! Guess who it is," I said. "It is the man who
has the greatest intellect in the world and who has
committed the greatest follies." "Can it be Mr. Fox?"
"Ah yes, himself." I shall have supper to-night with
him at the Neckers, with your ambassador and am-
bassadress; to-morrow he will have supper with me
with Mesdames de Luxembourg, de Cambis et Bois-
gelin, and the Chevalier de Boufflers.[1]

The next year Gibbon was in Paris, and
she brings forward his name as a further inducement to Crawford to come:

We have Mr. Gibbon here who will remain three or
four months. I am sure that he pleases you; I judge
by myself, I find him to have the best conversation;
he only arrived day before yesterday; I have already
had supper with him twice, I shall have supper with
him again to-morrow and the day after.[2]

Gibbon seldom inspired warm personal
regard and in later letters the writer reit-
erates that she finds him to possess plenty
of wit, but that she understands why he
is not better liked. George Selwyn was
equally at home in Paris salons and English

[1] *Correspondance complète de Madame Du Deffand,* ed. de M.
de Sainte-Aulaire, t. iii., p. 258.
[2] *Ibid.,* p. 266.

drawing-rooms, for he spent a part of each year in his early life in Paris, which he thoroughly appreciated. He and Madame Du Deffand were great friends; they, too, wrote to each other, and his name often occurs in her letters to others, with his *petit Milord*,[1] and the little Maria Fagniani,[2] his adopted Italian child, his relations with whom was the topic of the day in Paris as in London, and in whose absorbing affection every one sympathised: "I do not know any one so happy at this moment as Selwyn. No one can conceive so extravagant a passion as his, but it is very true."[3] Madame Du Deffand wrote in regard to this attachment. She admired English women and draws for Selwyn a charming portrait of the beautiful Lady Sarah Bunbury, who was at the time equally a belle in both capitals. She found Mrs. Damer,[4] probably in

---

[1] Frederic, Fifth Earl of Carlisle.

[2] Afterward Marchioness of Hertford. See George Selwyn: His Letters and his Life, ed. by E. S. Roscoe and Helen Clergue, London and New York, 1899, p. 8.

[3] *Correspondance complète de Madame Du Deffand*, ed. de M. de Sainte-Aulaire, t. iii., p. 356.

[4] The sculptress.

Paris on her way to or from Rome, *infini-ment aimable*. There is an admirable pic-ture, too, of Lady Pembroke. Indeed, she made friends with all the English ladies of note who visited Paris.

VI

But something more detailed must be said of the most charming, perhaps, of all Ma-dame Du Deffand's many friends in this epoch which was singularly rich in charming women. A stranger visiting Touraine is shown from the *allées* of the roof-garden of the château at Amboise, where François I liked to walk, across the silver Loire, a curi-ous columnar building, but faintly to be seen. It is the Chinese pagoda built by the Duc de Choiseul, and now the only archi-tectural remnant left of the estate of Chate-loup, the most magnificent private estab-lishment in Europe, the retreat sometimes of Madame Du Deffand, and the place of exile which the Duchesse de Choiseul willingly entered, because she could here enjoy, un-disturbed, the company of her too popular husband. For this was the pleasant land to which he was banished when, unwilling to join the party of Madame Du Barry, the Duke refused to accede to the King's request that he should be reconciled to her, and where the spectacle—extraordinary in France, which had always loved its kings—was daily beheld of the Court running to pay their respects to a disgraced minister. It is easy to imagine the life here in the sunshine, in the pretty, flat country watered by the Loire, the Cher, and the Indre, the laughing landscape of the pleasure-loving Rabelais.

In the Duchesse de Choiseul, Madame Du Deffand had a friend more worthy the name than any of the women with whom she was intimate. She has come down to us bright and perfect, standing forth a gracious and exquisite figure amid the too frequently tarnished portraits which form the gallery of the epoch. She was beautiful, clever, and good. She not only had the outward attributes of "a perfect little model"—as Walpole wrote to Gray—but she was also a pattern of propriety, of delicacy, tact, and womanly dignity. When very young she married a man who soon tired of the perfections of his wife, but all her life she vainly cherished the hope of winning his affection, and after his death she retired to a convent to save money to pay his debts. Convent-bred, she felt the narrowness and inutility of her education, and set herself to the task of being equal to her position as the wife of a public man. So complete and successful was the process of self-education which she undertook that at Rome, where her husband was sent as ambassador, the charming young French woman was admired and courted as much for her mental attainments as for her beauty and charm of character. Every one loved her, and she succeeded in holding to her ideal of conduct throughout a life spent in the gayest and most frivolous court in Europe to old age when, alone, she passed unscathed and unprotected through all the terrors of the French Revolution. Madame Du Deffand was her *confidante* in her painful endeavours to gain her husband's affection. In letters in which are plainly

visible the evidences of a sweet and strong
nature, we gain an insight into this pathetic
life history.   She begs, for instance, Madame
Du Deffand to say if the Duke had spoken
of her, and asks what he had said since her
last letter.   Her pride in him was as great
as her passion: " Let us confess that this
grandpapa is an excellent man ; but it is not
everything to be the best of men ; I assure
you that he is the greatest the century has
produced."[1]

The Duchess was twenty-five years
younger than Madame Du Deffand; their
friendship, perhaps, had an added warmth
from this disparity in years. Just as at the
same period there was a closer bond of
affection between George Selwyn, the famous wit and beau, and the Earl of Carlisle,
thirty years his junior, than perhaps could
have existed for more immediate contemporaries, so across the channel in France between two celebrated women, the older as

[1] Madame Du Deffand playfully called the Duc and Duchesse de
Choiseul grandpapa and grandmamma ; she was connected with the
family through her maternal grandmother, who was the stepmother of
the Duc de Choiseul.

famous a wit and as popular, the younger
also attractive and interesting and occupying
a high position, the same unusual association is seen, and their correspondence opens
up the same vista of uncommon minds in
easy and familiar and unstudied intercourse,
delightful to read in itself apart from its
historical interest.   Of a philosophical order
of mind, the letters of the Duchess reflect
the intellectual subtleties of the time; to her,
as to Madame Du Deffand, was denied the
solace of religious faith; unlike her, however,
she did not ceaselessly torment herself with
questions of a future state, but her more
serene temperament found contentment in
the enjoyment of nature and in service for
those about her; timid and gentle, she yet
knew how to maintain her opinions and her
dignity.   The Duchess possessed the elements that were wanting in Madame Du
Deffand and found in her friend's more
powerful nature a natural and congenial
opposite.   Monsieur Deschanels has struck
the note of contrast between these two
friends, and Monsieur Weiss has well said

on the same point: "Madame de Choiseul has in the character the charm which
her friend has in the intellect and she
has displayed in her conduct the justness
which the other practised only in her style."[1]

Madame Du Deffand held the right theory
of life, the Duchesse de Choiseul practised
it; and though her domestic relations were
not fortunate, she obtained happiness in
simple, healthy ways, and her sunny disposition, good mind, and warm heart made
her beloved by everybody—except her husband.

The French abbés of the eighteenth century were often more men of the world and
of affairs than ecclesiastics. We all know
how in the Abbé de Coulanges Madame de
Sévigné found her trusted man of business,
and a friend equally near to the Duc and
Duchesse de Choiseul and to Madame Du
Deffand was the Abbé Barthélemy. He had
rescued the Duke from a precarious position
at Court and, from the time of his marriage,

[1] *Essais sur l'Histoire de la Litterature Française,* J. J. Weiss,
Paris: Calmann Lévy, 1891, p. 347.

lived with him. This representative eight-eenth-century abbé, amiable, witty, agree-able, learned, mingling in the world and its joys and strifes, as well as pointing the way to heaven, turned from the brilliant, intel-lectual life to which he seemed destined by his unusual gifts to devote himself utterly to the care and happiness of "the gentlest little creature that ever came out of a fairy egg." So Walpole enthusiastically described the Duchess.[1]

Their life-long friendship, so productive of happiness for both, was a solace to the Duchess for the disappointment marriage had brought, and to the abbé for the loss of a career that had been the dream of his youth. And if he sometimes cast regretful glances backward towards that youth and its promise, in ministering to the sweet little Duchess he forgot its lack of fulfilment. To the last their friendship was unbroken, and when the Revolution drove her from the convent to which she had retired after the death of her husband, the good Abbé was

[1] *Letters of Horace Walpole*, ed. by Toynbee, vol. vi., Letter 1090.

the only visitor whom the delicate, frail little old woman received in the tiny apartment where she had taken refuge. Here he was seized and imprisoned by the general order, but she had the good fortune and the happiness of requiting his devotion by saving him from the guillotine.

VII

By the keenness of her judgment and the quality of her mind which was at the same time profound and brilliant, Madame Du Deffand has earned the right to be called the feminine Voltaire, and in the frequent conflicts of wit which we find in her correspondence with him she holds her own and, indeed, is often the victor. They were drawn together by a habit of mind strikingly similar. Their affectionate attachment, begun in youth, was lifelong, critical though it was on her part, and divided on his during his quasi-conjugal life with Madame Du Châtelet. When the philosopher, then become the "patriarch of Ferney," arrived in Paris, in 1778, he sought, to be sure, lodgings near Madame d'Épinay, but in this case affection for the later had not changed that for the earlier friend and he wrote at once to Madame Du Deffand, " I arrive dead, and I only wish to be resuscitated to throw myself at the feet of Madame Du Deffand." Madame Du Deffand, in spite of her fondness for Voltaire and d' Alembert, was never either in love or in league with the philosophers. After trying in vain to win her to their principles they, as a body, looked upon her with fear and did not lose an opportunity to do her an injury. Voltaire never ceased to urge her to join their ranks, well aware of the gain to them of so powerful a friend ; but she had nothing of the iconoclast in her disposition, and in return reproached him for the freedom with which he expressed his destructive opinions, and declared that she was by no means in sympathy with his disciples—that, on the contrary, she found them detestable, their hearts cold, their minds occupied with themselves. Fear was not included in her composition, and even the censure of Voltaire had no terrors for her.

As has been said, Madame Du Deffand's life contradicted her excellent judgment; against a passion for simplicity, for frankness, for truth and justice, a hatred for all deceit and affectation, were ranged in appalling strength a pressing need of variety, and an early satiety of every form of pleasure, of people, of amusements, of pursuits.

" I know that all men are vain and personal and that the best are those who are not envious and wicked and who are simply indifferent. I esteem no one, and I cannot escape from those whom I scorn."[1] A born sceptic is always a born critic, and Madame Du Deffand's analytical mind could not but measure the hearts, the brains, the motives of those about her—disenchantment was certain.   The spirit of scepticism and criticism kept her always doubtful of the sincerity of those dearest to her; of an enthusiastic temperament, she found no one worthy of devotion or sacrifice.   She divided society into three parts : *les trompés, les trompeurs*

[1] " Madame Du Deffand et sa famille," M. de Ségur, *Revue des Deux Mondes*, Nov. 15, 1906, p. 395.

et les trompettes!   Writing to President
Hénault, in 1742, from Forges, whither she
had gone to take the waters, she says : "As
for me, I am sorry not to see you ; but I
support it with a degree of courage, because
I believe that you do not share it much and
that it does not matter to you."[1] Even her
trust in the Duchesse de Choiseul is touched
by this blight : "you know that you love
me, but you do not feel it," she said one day
to her, a comment which led to many arguments on the subject between them, as we
see in this playful allusion : "Mr. Walpole
has written me a charming letter in which
he calls me also his grandmamma, because
he is your husband. . . . You were very
sorry to have him go, and I *felt* your concern much more than I *knew* it."[2]

Born in an age of doubt, Madame Du
Deffand, always quick to receive impressions, was early affected by the onward
movement, the rush of inquiry which,

[1] *Correspondance Complète de Madame Du Deffand,* ed. de
M. de Sainte-Aulaire, t. i, p. xlvii.
[2] *Correspondance Complète de Madame Du Deffand,* ed. de M.
de Sainte-Aulaire, t. i, p. 142.

during her lifetime, was sweeping over France. By nature an agnostic she was ever desiring to probe to the bottom of things ; to receive anything on trust seemed to her to be the part of ignorance. Yet all the time the possession of a personal living faith was the strongest desire of her heart. All her life she was longing for the peace which religion gives, and all her life it was denied her. She called to her help the most famous of the clergy, attended church, had her oratory, her confessor, studied the Bible. When she became blind she sought even more earnestly to find consolation in the Scriptures, but her mind was incapable of mysticism. "Eh! but can you understand anything in all that ?"[1] There was no sacredness in the tie of marriage to her, no reverence for religious ceremony of any kind, but nominally she belonged to the Church and, far from attacking, she always respected another's belief. "I was born melancholy, she wrote her sister, "inclined to sad reflec-

[1] *Correspondance Complète de Madame Du Deffand*, ed. de M. de Sainte-Aulaire, t. i., p. 20.

tions.   I have always wished very much
to be pious like you.   But wishes cannot
change our dispositions.   It is not any attachment for the things of the world which
turns me from devotion, it is my misfortune.
Pray God for me, my dear sister."[1]   She
was ready to receive light on things divine
or human, though without fixed moral principles to assist her.   To-day her acute mind
would have found more scope, and she
would have been a better and happier woman, because she would have found an object in life.   For what strikes us most in her
character is the incurable ennui from which
she suffered from childhood, and from which
she was always trying to escape at whatever
cost.   To a heart and an imagination, which
sometimes ran away with her reason, some
of the faults and many of the disappointments, and much of the wearisomeness of her
life may be attributed. Her wit was noted for
its biting edge, but if she were pitiless towards
others she was not just towards herself :

[1] " Madame Du Deffand et sa famille," par M. le Marquis de Ségur,
Revue des Deux Mondes, Nov. 15, 1906, p. 392.

I am sunk in the blackest reflections ; I have been thinking that I have spent all my life in illusions, that I have myself dug the abysses into which I have fallen, that all my judgments have been either false or reckless, and always too precipitate, that in fact, I have really never known any one, that I have not been known either, and that perhaps I have never known myself.[1]

French esprit is sometimes lacking in humour, and so it was with Madame du Deffand. Had she been given that sense which eases the jarring machinery of life and makes it work more smoothly, that lightening of the heart which comes from laughter, life would have seemed a less melancholy affair to this lonely woman. Madame Du Deffand experienced the truth of the saying of the old Greek, who proclaimed that he who pursues happiness will never find it. Without children or close family ties, by the very elevation of her intellect above the ordinary level about her, she felt singularly alone, and was possessed always by the mortal fear of being deserted by the bright but fickle world in which she had so long been a centre. This craze

[1] "Madame Du Deffand et sa famille," par M. de Ségur, *Revue des Deux Mondes*, Nov. 15, 1906., p. 396.

for companionship was not extraordinary
when we consider her physical condition.

I do not go to bed till one or two, I do not sleep,
I wait for seven o'clock with impatience ; my pen-
sioner arrives and he reads sometimes for four hours
before sleep comes ; when I sleep it is eleven or
twelve o'clock or often later still ; I do not get up till
five or six o'clock, at seven the visits begin, then supper, then loto.   There is a day gone, of which there
remains only regret to have employed the time so
badly, above all, when one reflects upon the little
which remains of it. [1]

Again she writes : "You do not know the
depression into which I fall when I think
of passing an evening alone. It is a *point
fixe* which I have in the head, a kind of
madness." [2]

Although every one shocked her, and
every one wounded her and bored her, she
was forced by this need of companionship
which had become an obsession to make incredible efforts not to break with every one.
And so, as she declined in years, her enter-

[1] " Madame Du Deffand et sa famille," par M. de Ségur, *Revue des
Deux Mondes,* Nov. 15, 1906, p. 400.
[2] " Madame Du Deffand et sa famille," par M. de Ségur, *Revue
des Deux Mondes,* Nov. 15, 1906, p. 396.

tainments were more carefully considered;
an ennuyée herself it was her constant aim
that others should not be bored. With this
object in view the table was laid, and feasts
material and intellectual were provided in
increasing abundance and delicacy to tempt
the jaded appetites of those for whom the
world held few novel delights. "Supper,"
she said one day, "is one of the four ends
of man. I do not recall" she added, iron-
ically, "the other three."[1] She who lived in
a time of decadence, in the conscious sadness of a soul which felt the impression of
that worn-out world which had lived too
much, partaken of forbidden fruit, and dying
from excess of knowledge, personified, too,
the human mind in quest of truth, of justice,
and of light.

It is evident that this is a portrait not of an
estimable woman or always of an amiable
character, but it is of one whose moral
weaknesses, as well as force of intellect and
social gifts, are an example of the epoch.

---

[1] *Correspondance complète de Madame Du Deffand* ed. de M.
de Sainte-Aulaire, t. i., p. 131.

Madame Du Deffand lived in the wrong century, a time which called out wit, the lighter faculties of the mind, and the practical questions which led to the Revolution ; the serenity, peace, faith, and aspirations in which the deeper characters and larger minds find sustenance, which bring forth the poet, were wanting in the eighteenth century.   In a later age, her capacity would have found freer outlet, and we should have seen a larger life, and labours in the world of literature, not more interesting to us it may be, but more satisfying to the mind and soul of the writer.   Madame Du Deffand has been called heartless, unfeeling, cold ; her letters prove her to have been passionate, sensitive, and sympathetic ; loving society but despising it, and equally bored with solitude, with her husband, with lovers, with herself.

MADAME D'ÉPINAY

1726. Birth of Louise Florence Pétronille d' Esclavelles, afterward Madame d'Épinay.

1745. Marriage.

1749. Beginning of intimacy with Francueil. Rousseau introduced. Foundation of salon.

1755. Rupture with Francueil. Beginning of intimacy with Grimm.

1756. Installs Rousseau in the Hermitage.

1757. Rupture with Rousseau. Departs for Geneva.
Meets Voltaire.

1759. Returns to Paris. Her circle enlarged.

1762. Obliged to give up the château de La Chevrette
and occupies La Briche.

1770. Obliged to give up La Briche and thenceforth
lives in different localities in Paris.

1783. Death.

MADAME D'EPINAY

I

THE influence of women in the society of France before the Revolution is one of the interesting features of the eighteenth century. It was an influence which was paramount, paradoxically enough, when they made no pretension to political power or to literary reputation, and it was obtained, not in competing with men, or by the exercise of masculine gifts, but by a brilliant display of essentially feminine qualities united to mental superiority. Their power was continuous and in a sense general, not confined to a particular group, but felt in a large section of society; for it was not one woman who attracted to her men and women of note, or the few who frequented the house of one remarkable woman; there was more than one salon and

more than one coterie ; but among them all
there was none more intellectually active
nor was there any woman who did more to
assist the forward movement of her time
than Madame d'Épinay.

The study contained in the previous pages
presents a woman so representative of the
highest social and intellectual plane of her time
that an appreciation of her and of her friends
is necessary for a complete realisation of the
age. The life of Madame d'Épinay is also
a history of a not less interesting phase of
that brilliant society of intellectual vivacity,
of splendid luxury, of social depravity, and
also of moral awakening. Though political
influence was never primarily the aim of the
salon, that of some women is a matter of
history. Madame Du Deffand, as I have
said, had no pretensions either as politician
or philosopher, yet her insight into affairs
more than once influenced the policy of
those in power of whom she was the friend
and the confidante. Although uneasily conscious of a sense of impending danger in
the popular thought to persons of her station

Madame d'Épinay

From the painting by Léotard in the Musée de Versailles

(By permission of Messrs. Neurdein)

Madame Du Deffand, like the ablest of those
about her, was surprisingly unappreciative
of the deeper movements of the age.   Aristocratic and exclusive, she turned away from
the innovations that characterised the last
half of the century and, though she possessed a mind of masculine power, her letters and a few fugitive verses alone are left as
a record of her understanding, her judgment,
and her wit.

Madame d'Épinay was a woman of altogether different character who, far from
strong-minded, needing guidance and easily
led, was ever under the sway of her emotions, yet she, also, possessed uncommon
intellectual gifts, the chief of which was
a keen observation to which was added
a power of literary expression.   Madame
d'Épinay obtained her reputation in philosophical, political, and literary circles through
the strength of her affections acting upon
a mind of singular brightness.   Her friends
aroused her interest in philosophy and politics, her children led her to the study of
education, on which she wrote, and which

brought her academic honours. Devoted to the philosophical sect, she gathered about her its different elements ; perceiving the trend of the reforms they advocated, farther sighted—perhaps by reason of the character of her friendships—than Madame Du Deffand, she prophesied the Revolution in a remarkable letter to the Abbé Galiani :

The suppression of the Cours des Aides is expected; the reason for haste is clear, and no one believes that their aim can be accomplished. Every one is troubled by this downfall of justice; every one rebels at the idea that the Council should be both judge and plaintiff. Great is the consternation. I see less disposition to violence than to desertion. Many think seriously of expatriating themselves; those who are bound by their position give vent to their distress by rant which helps nothing but which soothes. . . . Each step aggravates the ill. Every one is writing, every one will reply. . . . Every one will wish to dwell on the constitution of the State; heads will grow excited. Questions are raised which no one formerly would have dared consider. This is an irreparable ill. As I have said, my dear Abbé, these questions are the theology of administration. To be cleared up without danger, every man, by the result of his researches, must find himself as well treated and as happy as a reasonable being can hope; without which the knowledge acquired by the people must sooner or later produce revolution." [1]

While, then, eloquent discourses on friendship and love were led by Madame Du Deffand, politics, philosophy, and morality were the subjects which fixed attention on Madame d'Épinay's salon. Their grace, their wit, and their knowledge of mankind must always make these women charming companions, the more so because, with all their intellectual brilliancy, each is so much a woman whose heart and mind, though influenced by the corruption of her age, were constantly rebelling against it ; while understanding their weaknesses we can yet appreciate their endeavours and take delight in their company.

The early years of life usually determine its direction, and a knowledge of the influences to which she was subjected in childhood is especially important in order to appreciate the personality and career of Madame d'Épinay. Timid, irresolute, impres-

---

[1] *Derniéres Années de Madame d'Épinay,* par Lucien Pérey et Gaston Maugras.   Paris: Calmann Lévy, 1894, p. 420.

sionable, of quick perception and amiable disposition, she was peculiarly under the influence of her environment.

II

Louise Florence Pétronille d'Esclavelles, afterward Madame d'Épinay, was born on March 11, 1726. Her father, Baron d'Esclavelles, of an ancient and noble Norman family, was Governor of Valenciennes when, at the age of fifty-eight, he married Florence Angélique Proveur de Preux, of a noble family of Flanders, whose escutcheon, however, was sullied in the eyes of her husband's aristocratic kindred by the connexion of its bearers with finance. When his daughter was ten years old the Baron died, and she was left to the guardianship of his friend, the Comte d'Affrey, her beloved " tutor " and confidant, and of André Prouveur de Preux, a maternal uncle, a delightful, simple, and original character, whose acquaintance we owe to the *Mémoires* of Madame d'Épinay.

Baron d'Esclavelles leaving little behind him beside his honourable record, his widow was obliged to look to her relatives for assistance, and her sister, who had married Monsieur de Bellegarde, one of the richest farmers-general in the kingdom, then living sumptuously in a superb mansion on the rue St. Honoré, offered the widow and her child a home.

An elderly aunt, the Marquise de Roncherolles, a stranded relic of the old aristocracy, was the only remaining relative of the Baron. The Marquise had no home to offer but, although poor, she was lavish with the little fortune left her. Faithful to the old traditions, sheltered behind a convent's grating, she looked out upon the changing times with distrust and fear; but, if she were narrow in her ideas, she was warm in her sympathies. No one, however, was more scornful of the financiers among whom the rich connexions of her nephew's wife were enrolled and so it was natural that she should beg the Baroness to gather together the remnants of her scanty fortune, place her daughter with her in the convent, and solicit the king for a pension;

at all events, to decline Madame de Belle-garde's hospitality, which would alter their social position and ruin the child's prospect of a husband in her own rank of life.

But the Baroness, a little frightened by the aristocratic aunt's grand manner, pretensions, and prejudices, neglected to sue for the pension, and decided to accept her sister's invitation. It did not prove a happy choice. The Marquise alone, more appreciative than others of the character of Louise, not only loved her, but perceived the emotional temperament and quick intelligence which, in after life, was to make her house the meeting-place for the best intellects in Paris.

"You complain of her sensibility," she wrote, "but it is on the contrary a good gift from Heaven. I am sixty years old, I have seen the world, and I have never seen a sensitive nature turn out badly ; if she is badly led, she may err, but she will never be irredeemably lost." [1]

[1] *La Jeunesse de Madame d' Épinay*, par Lucien Pérey et Gaston Maugras. Paris : Calmann Lévy, 1898, p. 21.

Though Madame de Bellegarde was very rich, she was very mean. Jealous fears, moreover, were aroused, her clever and winning little niece attracting more attention than her own children and, in a few months, Louise was installed in a convent. She was taken away at the age of thirteen, and we have a description of her as she appeared at this time of her life to Monsieur d' Affrey : "Without being beautiful, she had a distinguished, noble, and touching appearance. Her features were wonderfully expressive. Her soul was painted in her innocent eyes which expressed as much candour as sweetness and intelligence."[1]

It was this interesting figure which, in the early summer of 1739, appeared at the château de La Chevrette, the magnificent country seat of Monsieur de Bellegarde, in the northern environs of Paris, the romantic setting of the first scene in the painful domestic drama of the life of our heroine.

The outline of the moat, the gate, the left

[1] *La Jeunesse de Madame d' Épinay*, par Lucien Pérey et Gaston Maugras. Paris : Calmann Lévy, 1898, p. 34.

wing, and some outbuildings are all that
now remain of the superb château. Built
in the grand siècle, it displayed all the splendour and ostentation of the old régime.   A
sketch of this interesting building drawn
by Monsieur de Francueil—whom we shall
meet—and engraved by Monsieur de Jully,
the second son of Monsieur de Bellegarde,
still exists. It rises stiff and stately, with
its long façade, square wings, and mansard
roof, from the midst of geometrical garden
beds, bordered by regular lines of trees ;
a fountain in an ornamental basin plays
in the foreground. Marble groups adorn
the shaded lawns, and the magnificent park,
containing the Hermitage lying concealed in
its outskirts, stretch away to the wooded
heights of Montmorency.

Louise early perceived her dependent
position in her aunt's household, and it was
not improved when one of her cousins
was discovered making love to her, for the
youthful La Live, the eldest son,[1] appre-

[1] Denis Joseph La Live de Bellegarde took the name of d' Épinay,
in 1741, from a title then acquired. He enjoyed all the rights and

THE CHÂTEAU DE LA CHEVRETTE.
After an Old Print by M. de la Live de Jully.

ciating the attraction of his cousin, had
lost no time in allowing his admiration
to be known. The boy and girl were at once
separated by their angry relatives, and the
gentle Louise promised, weeping, to give
up her young lover, but naïvely owned
that, following the direction of her confessor, she had offered prayers and gifts at
the altar that she should find a rich husband, and had undergone a *neuvaine* as a
thank-offering for the love of her cousin,
believing that she had, in both acts, fulfilled
her duties as a good Christian. Presently it
was learned that the priest had worked on
the mind of young La Live as well, with
the view of finally obtaining ascendency
over the entire family. The old Marquise,
to whom the thought of such an alliance
was even more offensive than to Madame
de Bellegarde, treated this matrimonial essay
with tact, and the young girl, who was suffering from shame and remorse, with much
kindness ; but at the same time she an-

privileges of the eldest son, though he had an elder brother, who,
being feeble-minded, was confined in a convent.

9

nounced that she would never give her
consent to a marriage between them unless
La Live should enter the army. The inheritance, however, of his father's profession
and the rich emoluments of his office were
not to be thrown away, and the young man
was sent on a tour of the provinces from
which the revenues were collected. But
presently, from time to time, came reports
of irregularities which augured ill for future
domestic tranquillity.

The death of Madame de Bellegarde, in
1740, again altered the current of the lives
of mother and daughter, for the Baroness,
who had taken Louise away, returned to
take charge of the bereaved family. The
shrouded mirrors, the sombre hangings, all
the grim spectacle that a French house in
mourning at that epoch presented, made a
vivid impression upon the sensitive girl,
who was not sorry when she was returned
to her convent.

Louise was nearly seventeen when she
again entered the family circle and drifted
helplessly toward a life for which nature had

ill fitted her to play an heroic part. Had she, however, been surrounded by good influences, the very traits which made her incapable of withstanding temptation would have been added charms in a character which possessed as a foundation many graces of spirit. But circumstances did not tend to upbuilding of character. La Live did not cease his attentions in his short visits to his home, but his cousin had already heard enough of his habits to be apprehensive of his future while her delicate position in the household was unwisely exaggerated by her mother until timidity and constraint gave rise to a want of frankness and sincerity from which she suffered all her life.

An advantageous marriage which was proposed at this time by a noble family, was declined, owing to the refusal of Monsieur de Bellegarde, who was probably influenced by an unconfessed prejudice for his son's inclination, to complete the dot, and young d'Épinay, now come into the property of that name, piqued that this proposition should even have been

considered, and aware of his cousin's growing hesitancy to regard him in the light of a
husband, invented tales of undermined
health, broken spirits, and a wasted life. His
schemes were not laid in vain ; the death of
his mother had removed the chief obstacle,
and Monsieur de Bellegarde soon gave his
consent. The marriage took place December
23, 1745.

III

The modern phase of the influence of
wealth now makes its appearance and men
who formerly carefully concealed the extent
of their riches, now found such prudence
unnecessary and, instead, boldly proclaimed
their right to a place in high society.

The farmers-general of the eighteenth
century were at the head of finance ; to
them was given the charge of all indirect
taxation, which they decided, fixed, and
collected ; there was supposed to be one
supreme director, but the post involved the
expenditure of such large sums that the
work was divided between many associates ;

some of their number made regular tours of the provinces to review and verify the revenues, and their selection and disposition were at the disposal of the Comptroller-General.

One of the scandals of the period was the extravagance of the men who held these offices, and Monsieur d' Épinay divided with Monsieur de la Popelinière the evil reputation of standing at the head of their associates in this respect. Though both were clever financiers, each squandered so much money and lived in such open violence of public opinion that Monsieur d' Épinay finally lost his lucrative post. The farmers-general not only held the first place in finance, but they occupied a unique position in society, though they did not yet enjoy the power which wealth now obtains, for many of the aristocracy still stood disdainfully aloof. They lived in the greatest luxury, worked with the philosophers, and drew about them the best that society afforded in cultivated minds.

The château de La Chevrette, as well as

the town house of the family, possessed
many art treasures, for a love of pictures, as
well as of music, was a marked characteristic
of Monsieur de Bellegarde, whose passion
and aptitude for the arts descended to his
children. Monsieur d'Epinay possessed his
share of this family heritage, but his æsthetic
tastes did not prevent him from having a
thoroughly bad moral character. He was
a dissipated spendthrift, an unkind son and
husband—he always professed to be fond of
his wife—though he somewhat disguised
these unpleasant features by cultivated and
agreeable manners.

The paramount influence that parents and
relatives maintain to-day in French families
is small compared with that which they
exercised at the time of which I am writing.
The newly married in eighteenth-century
France, unless possessed of large means,
had no separate establishment, and were as
much under the authority of parents as before
marriage. Old companions and new friends
could not be received without parental
sanction, their disagreements and discords

must be openly considered and settled in the family circle and if serious disputes arose between husband and wife, all their relatives were summoned, and the decision of this conclave was as binding as that of a court of law.

Madame d' Épinay was ever the creature of her emotions—sensibility was the link between herself and Rousseau—and, self-conscious, she was also harassed by the questionings of a sensitive conscience. Before her marriage her health had suffered from her anxiety to do her duty scrupulously and her wish to please every one exactly. Marriage did nothing to alleviate her situation. She tried to conceal her husband's late hours from their parents as if he were a school-boy, and if she remained out of the house longer than was expected she returned in terror, afraid of their reproaches.

It was a singular life, to our ideas, with little of the privacy which is valued so highly in the English family, but in which affection, perhaps, held as large a part, and where reverence for the authority of parents was a pleasing spectacle, if it sometimes proved an uncomfortable experience. But place an individual under such a system of espionage, whether in family life or at school, and character loses opportunity of growth, excess succeeds asceticism, calculated deceit follows extravagant confidences; or, if a submissive sweetness and an appealing gentleness be gained, these pleasing attributes too often are accompanied by a fatal weakness, and when the individual may have need of all his powers of resistance cultivated to their utmost and strengthened by habit and self-control, unaccustomed to self-reliance, he may find himself unfitted for the struggle of existence. This was the system under which Louise d'Épinay was educated and from which she suffered throughout her life.

Between the rigid rules of her mother, who held all places of amusement in horror, and the license of her husband, who would have led her into the most dissipated society of Paris, Madame d'Épinay was in constant difficulties. The glamour of the honeymoon was soon dispersed, and the bride, still in love with her husband, quickly had reason to complain of his neglect. To escape her reproaches, he threw her among unsuitable and even evil companions.

The unsophisticated wife was first introduced to Madame d'Arty, whose notorious connexion with the Prince de Conti does not seem to have compromised her in the eyes of society. She was followed by the most dangerous of the mondaines of Paris. Mademoiselle d'Ette, though "beautiful as an angel," was an intriguer. Introduced to Madame d'Épinay by her husband, she sought, under the guise of friendship, to detach her new friend from him, in order to place herself on a confidential footing and become indispensable in this rich household. Madame d'Épinay, ignorant of her true character, and deceived by her agreeable demeanour, confided to her the story of her unhappy married life. The lessons of this bad counsellor were not without results and, a real stage temptress, she moves across the scene, awakening doubt and followed by the practice of deceit and all the fatal consequences of perverted morals.

Throughout her life Madame d'Épinay felt the need for association with a stronger will, and it was largely through the influence of Mademoiselle d'Ette that her intimacy with Monsieur de Francueil[1] began.

In his extravagance and dissipation, Francueil nearly equalled Monsieur d'Épinay ; handsome, clever, and accomplished, he was known as an artist and musician at a time when a high degree of excellence was necessary for such a reputation, and to him must be given the credit of introducing to the house of Madame d'Épinay the celebrated men who formed her mind and made her salon famous.

Four years had passed since Madame d'Épinay's marriage. She had already lost her youthful freshness. Susceptible and sensitive, her health, never strong, was quickly affected by her mind, and disappointments and grievances had robbed her as well of her good spirits. In figure she was

[1] Francueil was the grandfather of George Sand.

small and thin, and the delicacy of her appearance was accentuated by an abundance
of dark hair, which grew prettily about her
temples and contrasted strikingly with the
extraordinary whiteness of her skin. Large
brown eyes, usually downcast, completed
a countenance which, though never beautiful and scarcely pretty, must have been
extremely interesting, for her seductive
charm is generally acknowledged. Though
mentally strong, she had no brilliantly attractive and quick imagination ; her mind
rather showed its power in its exactitude,
precision, and in the justness of her deci-
sions ; her ideas were slow in forming, nor
was she ready in their expression, restrained
not only by a natural slowness of speech,
but by an unconquerable reserve and
timidity.

Francueil was thirty-one ; petted, flattered, spoiled, but pleasing, he had only
to exert himself to make a conquest of the
entire family. He persuaded Monsieur de
Bellegarde to build a theatre at La Chevrette, for which he even gained the consent

of the austere Baroness, and organized a company which soon attracted the attention of society. Hither he brought Rousseau, who took part in his own plays. Duclos, the greatest gossip in the town, came to criticise, and remained in the hope of being enrolled among the players, his head turned by the captivating young hostess, while Gauffecourt, the delightful Genevan watchmaker, one of the popular idols, attached himself to Madame d' Épinay with a fidelity which never wavered. This was the nucleus and the beginning of one of the most memorable salons of the eighteenth century— a singular group, typical of the time, containing a most contradictory collection of personal qualities, and of which Madame d' Épinay was the greatest paradox.

IV

Paris, in that remarkable period between 1750 and the Revolution, was, in divers ways, cosmopolitan. Many distinguished Germans were settled there, whose names only reveal their foreign origin, so completely assimilated did they become with the forward movement produced by the great intellectual activity of their adopted country. German officers were popular, and German discipline was urged in the reforms of the army.

The Comte de Schönberg and his relative, the brilliant and prodigal Comte de Friesen, were favourites in the salons, and Grimm and d'Holbach added, both by talent, the latter by hospitality as well, to the prestige of men of letters in Paris. Grimm, disappointed at the failure of his literary début after leaving the University of Leipzig, had come to France as tutor to the sons of the Comte de Schönberg. Rousseau, attracted to Grimm by his interest in music, introduced him to the Encyclopédistes, and he obtained the post of secretary to the Comte de Friesen. From that time his success was assured, and he was admitted to the best society of Paris. Gauffecourt called him " Tyran le Blanc," a term which contained a double meaning, relating as it did both to his character and to his complexion, for he painted his cheeks with white lead.

Baron Friederich Melchior Grimm[1] belonged to a characteristic Saxon type—tall, loose-jointed, with prominent eyes. He was indolent, indifferent, and ill at ease, with all the brusqueness and hardness of fibre of his race. He was always authoritative without being always correct, and though not devoid of sympathy, was without sensitiveness. Grimm inspired confidence without giving it; he possessed penetration, but at the same time he was slow and dull. Obsequious toward those in authority, the epithet of "Tyran" could only be applied in the case of those who, like Madame d'Épinay, depended on him; Catherine II objected as vigorously to his "prosternations" as she had hitherto done to those of Madame Geoffrin. When his jealousy or prejudices were aroused Grimm was not an impartial judge; he has been

[1] Grimm was of bourgeois origin, obtaining his title in 1775 when he was made minister plenipotentiary to the Court of France by the Duc de Saxe Gotha.

GRIMM.

After the Drawing by Carmontelle.

called, nevertheless, the best critic that the century produced, but he lacked the sacred fire, the life-producing seed; of creative genius he had none.

Contrasts in character as were Grimm and Madame d' Épinay, it was this very difference which produced her reliance upon him. According to the *Mémoires*, their intimacy had its origin in a romantic adventure. One evening at the house of the Comte de Friesen, Madame d' Épinay's reputation was violently assailed, and Grimm, whom Rousseau had but lately introduced to her, gallantly took up her defence.

I have had the honour of meeting Madame d' Épinay. . . . She is intelligent, they say that she does much good, that she is high-minded and generous. No one can persuade me that in twenty-four hours habits and principles can be changed and all the advantages which an honest person enjoys be sacrificed for interests so mean.[1]

The discussion, however, still went on, and became so violent that the participants descended to the garden, where a duel was

[1] *Mémoires de Madame d'Epinay*, par M. Paul Boiteau. Paris : Bibliothèque-Charpentier, 1891, t. i., p. 446.

fought, and Grimm was wounded. Soon afterwards the Baron, now become a hero, accompanied d'Holbach on a journey of some months' duration, but he did not leave Paris before seeing Madame d'Épinay, who, with Madame d'Esclavelles, received him warmly, and on his return he was welcomed as an old friend.

But the fact that Madame d'Épinay had found a defender did not save her from further hostile criticism. Duclos, Voltaire's successor as historian of France and a man who was made much of in society where his rude wit amused, attempting to supplant Francueil in Madame d'Épinay's affections, perceived Grimm's rising influence with increasing dislike. His behaviour at last, the lady claimed, became insupportable,[1] and she refused him admittance to her house, a proceeding which became the subject of considerable gossip all over the town. Francueil, also, by his reckless follies, had lost her good opinion, and, in spite of

[1] *Mémoires de Madame d'Épinay*, par M. Paul Boiteau, t. ii., p. 77.

her popularity, Madame d'Épinay was not happy. "Young, rich, interesting, witty, and charming," as Grimm depicts her at this time of her life, she yet had good reason to feel dissatisfied, and turned her thoughts to the religious life, the refuge of so many women who were weary of the world.

But fortunately her confessor was neither the typical worldly abbé of the eighteenth-century nor was he the ascetic ecclesiastic, dead to all interests save those of the Church. The one might possibly have offered himself as a consoler, the other have taken her income. The religion of abbé l'Martin was of another quality. Instead of taking advantage of her weakness, he directed her to fulfil her duties to her family and to society. "I see, Madame, that you are going to use God as a makeshift. If a person despises the world when he forsakes it for God, it may as well be said that he who enters the world despises God."[1]

Madame d'Épinay was obliged to ac-

[1] *Mémoires de Madame d' Épinay*, par M. Paul Boiteau, t. i., p. 366.

knowledge the force of the reasoning of the good abbé, and again, though somewhat sadly, gathered up the tangled threads of her life. That life we must not judge from the standards of to-day; Madame d'Épinay and her friends would now be as amazed as ourselves at the license then tolerated.

Society among the upper classes was composed of men and women absolutely without occupation. Parents of any position saw little of their children, who were taken from their mother at birth and given in charge of a foster-mother till the age of five, when they were sent to college or to a convent until a marriage was arranged. Practical politics, as we know them, did not then afford a career any more than business. There were no such resorts as Brooke's and White's that flourished across the Channel; the *cercle* of the boulevards of to-day had not come into existence. Unlike the Englishman, too, who likes to be by himself, and amuses himself with sport, the Frenchman enjoys society and the companionship of women. So, in Paris, men and women spent their time together in the stimulating atmosphere of the salons, at public balls, at the theatre or the gaming-table.

A predilection for country life, however, is a feature of the period, and the different coteries would meet at their grand châteaux where, with little outside themselves to divert them, they sat in their stately, cold, somewhat empty, though magnificently decorated salons, the women at the embroidery frame, the men sketching; sometimes they read aloud, and chess was a favourite game; for the evening a concert might be arranged, or a comedy—written by one of the company—but exercise was generally limited to walks in the straight garden paths or through the leafy lanes of the ancient parks.

In many respects it was an ideal state of society. Men and women were not separated; their aims and interests were identical, and they joined in the same pursuits, while practice in the art of pleasing had developed a careful observance of the amenities which brighten existence. A charming courtesy was the rule in behaviour, antipathies and prejudices were softened or conquered, sarcasm was frowned down as a needless weapon for wit, and discussion never degenerated into dispute. Manners were easy and gracious, yet dignified; the timid were given confidence, the reserved were drawn out, support was given without the appearance of patronage. As the century wore on Rousseau set the fashion for simplicity, and the graver tone of thought did not extinguish the gay, light good-humour thrown over the fundamental seriousness of the Latin race. It was a state only to be reached under the conditions then existing, and by a people of special instincts, tastes, and of special intellectual development. It created a society which was acknowledged throughout Europe as, in outward aspect at least, a pattern of elegance, sobriety, and amiability.[1]

In this odd mixture of ideas and ideals the sole purpose of marriage was for establish-

---

[1] *La Femme au Dix-Huitiéme Siécle*, par Edmond et Jules de Goncourt. Paris: Bibliothèque-Charpentier, 1896, p. 64.

ment ; for a woman it was the only means by which she could benefit from society ; congenial personality was hardly considered, and a man and wife in love were a ridiculous anomaly, not only uncommon, but rather shocking to the taste which formed the moral code.

The study of the period brings forcibly before us the remarkable change that society has since undergone, and it was largely the ideas which these very men and women of whom I am writing evoked and spread which provoked and supported the Revolution, when old forms fell forever and modern society, with its theories, reforms, and practices, came into being.

Monsieur de Bellegarde, foreseeing that his son would eventually ruin his family, had settled an income on Madame d' Épinay and her children but, though Monsieur d' Épinay and his wife were now practically separated, he continually annoyed her by demands for money, which she seldom had the strength of mind to refuse. Her troubles had already begun to affect her health, but she had the consolation of her children whom, contrary to custom, she personally looked after and whose education was her chief pleasure and interest. Her friends, too, occupied a large place in her life, making up in a measure for some of its disappointments. Grimm, Rousseau, Saint-Lambert, Desmoulins, and Gauffecourt, her "five bears," were her constant companions. A long epistle in verse, addressed to Grimm at about this time, playfully begins :

> Moi, de cinq ours la souveraine,
> Qui les donne et prescrit des lois,
> Faut-il que je sois à la fois
> Et votre esclave et votre reine,
> O des tyrans les plus tyran.[1]

V

A woman who has been characterised as "the best endowed and the most sweetly excellent of her epoch," the heroine of Rousseau's famous romance, the Comtesse d'Houdetot, youngest of Monsieur de Bellegarde's children, was also connected

[1] *La Jeunesse de Madame d' Épinay*, par Lucien Pérey et Gaston Maugras.　Paris : Calmann Lévy, 1898, p. 437.

with Madame d' Épinay's salon, and is intimately associated with some of the most interesting episodes of her life.

The Countess possessed that indefinable human quality, that subtle, sympathetic birthright, to which is given the name of charm. The spell that she wielded over her contemporaries proceeded from disposition, character, and mind, for she was altogether without personal beauty. Fragonard painted her, and we are disappointed. Her eyes are round, a signal defect in the time of the Bourbons, the beauty of whose almond-shaped eyes was so celebrated, and her sight was so bad that she was uncertain in her movements, but intelligence, good feeling, and refinement lent beauty to her expression. She had, besides, the gift of good-humour; cheerfulness and gaiety surrounded her wherever she moved; even a marriage without love could not quench her good spirits. There must have been something peculiarly appealing and winning in this union of heart and mind which could arouse the passionate love of Rousseau and gain the untiring devotion of the cool and fastidious Saint-Lambert.

Rousseau has immortalised her. The story of his passion turned the eyes of the world upon her and since that time of storm and stress, when, in the moonlit night, beneath the delicately drooping, heavily scented boughs of the acacia tree, we dimly descry her and hear the tender declarations fall trembling from the lips of the eloquent philosopher, the passing teamster's rude cry, her laughter, his ejaculation of despair, *l' amitié* and *l' amour*—competing sentiments throughout the century—contending with one another, she has held a place amid the remarkable portraits of that singular epoch—the period between 1750 and the Revolution.

Madame d'Houdetot's marriage was arranged with a promptitude remarkable even for those days. It contained, to begin with, a tragic element of discord, for the Comte d'Houdetot, whom Madame d'Épinay—though she probably exaggerated his weak points—describes as "a gambler by profession, ugly as the devil . . . in a word, unknown, and made to be so,"[1] had irrevocably bestowed his affection on another. But, determined to be happy, Madame d' Houdetot, who certainly was never in love with her husband, made the best of the situation and by her behaviour won his respect and admiration. He left her entire liberty and they were the best of friends, if nothing more, throughout their long lives.

The Salic law still distinguished between the sexes, and a woman on her marriage was lifted or fell into her husband's position in society. Madame d' Épinay, for example, by her marriage, descended from the rank which was hers by birth, and lost her right to social recognition at Court where, by the same law of etiquette, her sister-in-law gained admittance and even became a friend of the Queen, Marie Leczinska.

The Countess was soon allied with many celebrated people and entered into that ex-

[1] *Mémoires de Madame d' Épinay*, par Paul Boiteau. Paris : Bibliothèque-Charpentier, t. i., p. 101.

clusive company to be found at the house
of the Maréchale de Beauvau, whose salon
rivalled that of the Maréchale de Luxembourg in distinction, and whose lovable
qualities equalled the Countess' own.

Madame Necker's country house at Saint-
Ouen was near La Chevrette, in Madame
d'Houdetot's familiar country. They met
at Madame d'Épinay's theatre, and conceived a friendship for each other, in which
little Germaine, the future Madame de Staël,
was included. When Madame Necker went
to Spa for the waters, the Countess
kept her informed of the progress of the
child, with whom, as soon as she was old
enough, she began a correspondence. These
letters, some of which still exist, show
something of the degree to which Madame
d'Houdetot interested herself in those she
loved.

The lifelong attachment of Madame
d'Houdetot to Saint-Lambert is one of the
curious episodes of the time. Madame Du
Deffand stigmatises the work of the poet
as cold, thin, sterile, worn out; but if cold,

he was polished, and if his nature lacked
depth, warmth, and fertility, he was elegant, exquisite, and delicate ; and Madame
d' Houdetot clung steadfastly to a friend
who possessed, from this time of his life, at
any rate, the merit of constancy. And Saint-
Lambert had many mental attractions. To
the charm of simplicity he added a keen
love of nature, which he faithfully studied.
Both were poets. The *Saisons,* his celebrated pastoral—celebrated, at least, in his
time—struck the popular note. Madame
d' Houdetot's verses never reached the general public, though she acquired such a
literary reputation in her accomplished
world that Marmontel calls her the " Sévigné
de Sannois."

A reputation in the salons was not easily
obtained by a newcomer even with talents
and social recognition. Fastidious Madame
Du Deffand, when she first met Madame
d' Houdetot and Madame Necker, rather
scoffingly alludes to the occasion. " I have
made the acquaintance," she said, " of Madame Necker, I supped yesterday with Mes-

dames de Marchais and d'Houdetot. I was saying to myself all the while; what business had I to get myself into this mess? The fear of being bored makes one throw oneself into the water for fear of the rain."[1]

But as her visits to Madame Necker were continued, she must have changed her mind, and Madame d'Houdetot found the world as a rule well disposed even before she had become celebrated as Rousseau's "Sophie." Maria Edgeworth, who met the Countess at the house of l'Abbé Morellet, tells us that she possessed the priceless gift of seeing the good side of everything; and Madame d'Épinay, in spite of some jealousy when Rousseau's passion for her sister-in-law caused him to neglect his older friend, completes her *Portrait* in these significant words: "She never either spoke or believed ill of any one, and whoever undertakes to criticise her will end like me by praising her."

Franklin and Jefferson were frequently among the guests at Sannois, the Countess's

---

[1] *Correspondance complète de Madame Du Deffand*, ed. de M. de Sainte-Aulaire, t. ii., p. 466.

country seat. On Franklin's first visit he
brought an acacia from Virginia, and its
planting was celebrated as an international
event. Verses composed by the hostess
who, with her husband, met him on his
entrance to the village, were sung during
the ceremony. At the feast which followed,
each one recited an improvised verse in the
American's honour, signalling the attitude
of the noblesse toward Republican principles, and at his departure the Countess's farewell was phrased in the same
complimentary and poetic form :

Legislateur d'un monde, et bienfaiteur des deux
L'homme, dans tous les temps, te devra ses homages,
    Et je m'acquitte dans ses lieux
    De la dette de tous les ages.

The reader may be disposed to smile at
this somewhat stagey scene and its palpable
effort after effect, but the high-sounding
phrases were merely the fashion of the day
and events gave proof of their intrinsic sincerity. Without doubt the Countess manifested
exceptional sympathy with the American
revolutionists, for in 1775 she received citi-

zenship from the town of New Haven, together with her friends, Saint-Lambert, the
Maréchal de Beauvau, Condorcet, and other
eminent Frenchmen, distinguished (the report reads) not only by their rank, their
lights, and their talents, but by their philan-
thropy, and by their zeal for the liberty and
the happiness of the United States in general, and for the prosperity of New Haven in
particular.

A few words relating to Madame d'Houdetot's old age may not be uninteresting.
Retaining her interest in people and in
events, she passed unharmed through the
Revolution and saw the First Empire in-
augurated, an exemplar, in the new régime,
of the elegance of the old, agreeable society,
and of the art of conversation as it existed
in its best period. Madame de Rémusat
was of a later generation, but she used to
meet Madame d'Houdetot at her mother's
house—their lands adjoined—and she has
left us some idea of the warm regard which,
at this time of her life, Madame d'Houdetot
inspired.

Kindness, I will not say goodness, could not be carried farther than by Madame d' Houdetot. Goodness requires a sort of discernment of evil; it is seen and pardoned. Madame d' Houdetot has never observed ill in any one. We have seen her suffer in this regard, suffer really, when the least fault was found before her. . . . Her warm feelings have prolonged the period of youth.[1]

Deprived by death of her husband and of Saint-Lambert, she formed once more a deep attachment. Monsieur de Sommariva, a scholarly Italian, had become her neighbour by the purchase of La Chevrette from Madame d' Épinay. He was young enough to be the Countess's son, but in spite of years, she succeeded in inspiring a new devotion, and daily attentions and gifts of flowers kept alive the old romantic traditions for her who typified throughout her long life the amenities and affections.[2]

Rousseau's connection with this lady, the very crux of his emotional inner life, as of his fame, fortune, and career, began in the spring of 1756. He had reached middle

[1] *La Comtesse d' Houdetot*, par Hippolyte-Buffenoir. Paris: Calmann Lévy, 1901, p. 77.
[2] Madame d' Houdetot outlived most of her contemporaries. Her death occurred January 28, 1813.

life, but this was the stormiest episode of his troubled existence. Subdued by Madame d'Épinay, he was installed in the ancient Hermitage on the borders of the park of the château de La Chevrette, within reach of friends, but well withdrawn from the unendurable din of Paris. Satisfied with the glory he had achieved, his love of independence, his hatred of obligation, for a time lay sleeping. The freedom of the country was his to enjoy; his sensuous love of nature was gratified. It was April; vegetation was springing to life, and the symbols of spring were repeated in the fresh colours of morning and in the dewy evening; existence was a harmony of dreamy, languid days, of cool and quiet nights. Never since his early life amid the mountains of Savoy had Jean Jacques led a tranquil life, and he now revelled in a luxury of solitude, broken only by those whom he loved, for his closest friends were near, seemingly anxious to devote themselves to his welfare and to shower upon him the caresses which he craved.

JEAN JACQUES ROUSSEAU.
After a Drawing by Mauzaisse.

The Seven Years' War, which lost Canada
to France, entered upon because Frederick
of Prussia had offended Madame de Pompadour, had at this time (1757) begun. The
Comte d' Houdetot and Saint-Lambert were
off to the frontier. The Countess was established at Eaubonne ; here she was near La
Chevrette and not so far from Paris but that
she could also mingle in the diversions of the
Court. One morning she bethought herself of Rousseau, now her neighbour. She
had met him on the eve of her marriage ;
he had become more famous with the pas-
sage of time, and she determined to pay him
a visit. By some freak—perhaps in thought
of his eccentricities—dressed in man's garb,
she arrived at his door on horseback, laughing, excited by the dangers of the bad roads
she had passed over. Taken completely
unawares by this animated, high-spirited
Diana, Rousseau fell in love at first sight.
For the next few quickly flying weeks their
intercourse was daily ; its pretended motive,
conversations on subjects with which, indeed, Rousseau's brain and heart were filled

—the converting of society, the uplifting of humanity, its return to simplicity, to truth, to nature.

The sequel to these sentimental meetings, to the congenial intellectual companionship, and to the adoration which the charming Countess inspired, was the inception of *Julie*, the great romance which crowned Rousseau's fame. Madame d' Houdetot, transfigured in his imagination, is his heroine. But his poor servant, the foolish Theresa, jealous of these frequent interviews, carried reports of the sudden intimacy to Madame d' Épinay, who, as well as Theresa—so the *Mémoires* pretend—was accused of writing an anonymous letter which Saint-Lambert was said to have received, setting forth the conduct of Rousseau and of Madame d' Houdetot in an unfavourable light.

Diderot—according to his friends—anxious to put an end to the coolness which had naturally sprung up between Rousseau and Saint-Lambert, only sought, though with overmuch zeal, to advise Rousseau as to the course he should pursue. But Diderot's good

faith in all that relates to Rousseau has been
brought into question and, were his motives as honourable as he professed, his was
an unfortunate method to pursue with the
erratic and self-willed philosopher, so jealous
of his liberty of action. The peculiar temperament with which he had to deal, the
extreme sensitiveness, the perhaps unreason-
able pride, the timidity born of fear lest
it should be impossible to keep body
and soul together, should have been taken
into account. Hard experience had left
Rousseau mistrustful, reserved, and with
a hatred of authority, while deep seated
in his nature lay an over-powering self-
consciousness which, after the discovery
that his friends had once betrayed him,
made him suspicious of every human being.
Both Diderot and Grimm proclaimed that his
warm affections, added to their admiration
for his genius, alone retained those whom
his variable humours and vagaries must
long since have chased from him ; Diderot even complained that straightforward
methods were not to the taste of the hermit

philosopher who, on the other hand, publicly accused Diderot of publishing broadcast his most private concerns and of abusing his most sacred feelings. And further complications arose. Diderot sending his latest play to the Hermitage for criticism, Rousseau saw in the preface an allusion to himself which he considered offensive. With great difficulty Madame d'Épinay succeeded in calming his resentment and a rupture, for the time, was avoided.

But disunion in such a group, once begun, was certain to continue. The departure of Madame d'Épinay, in 1757, for Geneva, in search of health, was the occasion of a further weakening of the bonds which had for so long and so productive a period bound together these famous persons in comradeship.

Rousseau had not long before talked of returning to his birthplace, and would undoubtedly have done so had not Madame d'Épinay by her act of hospitality kept the author of *Julie* and *Émile* in France and thus added to the glory of French letters.[1] He was now asked to accompany her, and it was pointed out to him that gratitude toward his benefactress made acquiescence a duty.

But Rousseau did not see his duty in the same light as did these advisers. Out of health himself, he considered that he was the last person in the world fit to look after another invalid. Whereupon the friends called him a monster of ingratitude. The affair reached its climax when Rousseau published *La Lettre à d' Alembert contre les Spectacles*, which, as it attacked the stage, was considered an open declaration of war against the *encyclopédistes*, who advocated theatrical representations. Of this publication Madame d' Épinay, now in Switzerland, harassed in body and mind, learned with pain, realising that all hope of reconciliation was at an end. She never saw Rousseau again.

So, too, he passed out of Madame d'Houdetot's life, though they preserved affection-

---

[1] Though Rousseau was born in Geneva, he was of pure French extraction.

ate recollections of one another, and both she and Saint-Lambert afterward offered him a home and always defended him in the unhappy course of his life which followed. At Sannois, on a pedestal designed expressly for them, could be seen the two volumes of *La Nouvelle Héloïse* which Rousseau copied in his own hand for Madame d'Houdetot, and his four famous letters on *Virtue* and *Happiness* are addressed to her, who evoked an ideal type, a model of the homely virtues. Their relations with Rousseau would, alone, make Madame d'Houdetot and Madame d'Épinay forever interesting and, at a later period, the story of their friendship and its stormy conclusion was revived by his *Confessions* and by her scarcely less realistic *Mémoires*.

VI

It is to be noted that the intellectual Frenchwomen of the eighteenth century thought much and wrote much and well on the subject of education. They felt keenly the want of a guiding principle, the need of

a more substantial foundation than was to
be found in the prevailing system; an
education that would achieve something
more than agreeable manners, something
beside Latin verse, even beyond Greek
philosophy—a training which would lead
to growth of character. Madame d' Épinay
perceived the difference between education
and instruction, and declared that the public school could not take the place of the
family.

Madame Du Deffand never ceased to de-
cry the education of the times, to which
she ascribed all the misfortunes and evils of
her life. Madame d' Épinay, the mother of
two children, and devoted to their welfare,
had even more reason to consider this question important. With the birth of children
had come differences with her family because of the wish to keep them with her,
and she found it well-nigh impossible to
over-ride the fashion which made it almost
obligatory to rear children away from home.

In the meantime her mind was develop-
ing, and her own education—for she was

still young—which was to fit her for the
leadership of a salon, was in progress. No
woman of ordinary endowment or attainments could hope to occupy such a position
in French society. She who aspired to a
salon needed not only an educated but a
trained and critical faculty. She must be
able, not only to talk herself, but to open
the lips, as well as the minds, of others.
And no person, no matter how distinguished, was expected to enter the house
of a *bel esprit* unless he added to the general entertainment; even a prince, if he
could not shine himself, must do his part by
providing a substitute.[1]

In 1754 we first gather that Madame
d' Épinay began to write on the subject that most appealed to her; but it
is in her letters to her children that her
interest in education rises to enthusiasm
and they are the beginnings of her educational works. The first letters which were
composed for her son's edification were
beyond any child's comprehension; fortu-

[1] *Mémoires de Madame d'Épinay*, t. i., p. 381.

nately, however, for the little boy, Rousseau, whose advice on the matter was solicited, came to his rescue and the correspondence was placed more on a level with a child's intelligence.

"You have asked my advice in writing, Madame, here it is. . . . I think that the idea of writing him is a very happy one and may have a good influence; but two conditions are necessary—they are that he is able to understand you and that he is able to reply. These letters should be written for him alone, and the two that you have sent me would be good for all the world except for him. . . . Of what use is it, for example, to instruct him concerning your duties as a mother? Why cry in his ear the words submission, duties, vigilance, right ? All that has a frightful sound at his age. . . . Your definition of politeness is just and delicate, but it is necessary to think twice to appreciate it. Does he know what you mean by esteem, by benevolence ? Is he in a state to distinguish the voluntary or involuntary expression of a sensible heart ?"[1]

In Madame d'Épinay's description of the visit which she paid with Duclos to her son and his tutor at the Collège du Plessis the faults of the system in vogue are unmercifully exposed. They find the tutor, whom they interviewed on his method of pedagogy,

[1] *Mémoires de Madame d'Épinay*, t. ii., p. 23.

taking his ease, stretched at full length
on a couch, wig off, in dressing-gown; while
the child is seated at a table making aimless
marks with a pencil, unable to grasp the
difficult Latin task set before him.

In June, 1757, we find Madame d'Épinay
established in her favourite country house,
the château de La Chevrette. Her mother,
her children, the Comtesse d'Houdetot, and
Saint-Lambert were with her; Grimm, who
had now taken Francueil's place, was a frequent visitor; she was surrounded by all
those whom she loved.

Her life at this period had taken, in a
measure, the form which it retained to its
end. Her days at the château, where the
most of her time was passed, were seldom
wanting in the company of some of the brilliant coterie whom, aided by Francueil and
Grimm, she had gathered around her. Intermingled work and play, the joy of toil,
the happiness of intellectual labour and
achievement, was their task and their pleasure. Rousseau, comfortably installed at the
Hermitage, was her constant companion and

teacher. Generous, inexacting, forgiving, even the wilful, liberty-loving philosopher could receive her benefits and suffer her gentle control. D'Holbach had turned from disparagement to praise. Diderot, alone, of those she would have liked to count among her friends, in spite of Grimm's efforts, still held aloof.

But now, when she had adjusted her life as she thought she best could to its conditions and when a measure of tranquillity seemed to be established, her health, which had been continually failing, gave way, and it was decided that she must go to Geneva to be under the care of the eminent surgeon Tronchin. It was at this time also that Rousseau, of whom, in his fever for the society of Madame d'Houdetot, she had lately seen little, harassed past endurance, both by his so-called friends and his conscience, turned, as has been related, from her and from all the late harmonious circle, and the ties formed by years of helpful intercourse were quickly sundered.

But though Madame d'Épinay lost an

illustrious friend in Rousseau, she presently gained another in Voltaire. Accompanied by her husband and son the interesting invalid arrived in Geneva early in November, 1757, with a European reputation. She was received with every mark of attention by Rousseau's countrymen and by Voltaire who, though no longer young, was still inspired to write verses to the "*grands yeux noirs*" of the charming exile. At the time of her arrival, Voltaire, now at the height of his fame, had not yet bought Ferney, but inhabited Les Délices, a charming country house near the city, cared for and idolised by the absurd and good-natured Madame Denis, the niece whom "he cherished, mocked, and revered."[1]

Voltaire was indeed overjoyed to have the celebrated Frenchwoman in his neighbourhood, but Madame d'Épinay, whom the hardships of the journey had brought very near death, and who had received the sacraments, was reluctant to fraternise so soon with the arch-enemy of the Church, and de-

[1] *Mémoires de Madame d'Épinay*, t. ii., p 421.

BARON D'HOLBACH.
From a Portrait in the Musée Condé, Chantilly.

clined his first advances. "Having confessed
and received communion two days before,
I did not find it seemly to dine with Voltaire two days afterward," she wrote. But
Voltaire, who never did anything by halves,
was not to be denied. He became more and
more assiduous in his attentions, and show-
ered notes and invitations upon " *la véritable
philosophe des femmes*," as he called her,
and if he were attracted by her mind he admired also the amiability which her suffer-
ings could not destroy, and her soft, dark
eyes still had power to cast a spell over a
philosopher. When, the winter coming on,
Voltaire removed to Lausanne, he missed her
so much that he felt obliged to write frequently. "We are filled with regret to have
left her and with remorse not to have gone to
Geneva ; we ask her forgiveness. We could
wish three or four years of languor for the
true philosopher that she might have need of
four years of the great Tronchin. . . . Ah !
if she could come to Lausanne!" He did not
cease to press her to visit him, his zeal perhaps
the keener in his hope also to secure Tron-

chin, for whom he had a great admiration
and who was difficult of persuasion. Madame d' Épinay's esteem for her physician
increased daily. Voltaire she called her
nourisson, but Tronchin was her *sauveur*,
and she marked her gratitude by having her
portrait painted for him by the celebrated
Liotard.[1]

Although he had no theatre at Lausanne
such as Ferney afterward boasted, Voltaire,
in order to produce his plays, had a stage
fitted up wherever he might be. His guests
and his friends were drawn in as actors, and
he also obtained professionals from Paris.
He therefore, in his efforts to obtain her
company, brought forward his theatre as
the first inducement he had to offer, but,
still unsuccessful, he tried other expedients,
and finally accused her of deserting him for
the orthodox party, who had pronounced
against his defence of Lord Bolingbroke, an
accusation which at last brought her and
Tronchin to reassure him.

[1] This portrait is in the museum at Geneva, and a copy, done at
the same time, is at Versailles.

But, though Madame d'Épinay was gratified by so many proofs of regard from Voltaire and by the manifold attentions shown
her in Geneva, she was homesick, and Grimm,
at work with Diderot revising the first volumes of the *Encyclopédie,* continued to defer
his promised visit till a crisis in her health
at last brought him in the spring of 1759.
She became, however, so much better during
the summer that she was able to return to
Paris in the autumn with him and her brother-
in-law, Monsieur de Jully, who was also
leaving Switzerland, disappointed in his
diplomatic mission for Madame de Pompadour,[1] who had been scheming to obtain
the sovereignty of Neufchâtel.

VII

This year marks an important point in the
life and career of Madame d'Épinay. She
was yet only thirty-three, but she had
learnt much. Her long absence offered
opportunity for any changes she might wish
to make in her mode of life, and, taught by

Madame de Pompadour was related to the d'Épinay family.

experience, she was long in forming her new salon, for which her delicate health was an excellent excuse. Voltaire's attentions had added to the reputation which she had already achieved and now, too, her wish that Diderot should become her friend was at last gratified and his friendship, if slow in making, was deep and lasting. Not long afterward he significantly wrote from La Chevrette: "The day after to-morrow I am established at Grandval for six weeks; Madame d'Épinay is a little heavy-hearted on account of it, I also; we understand each other without saying a word; we blame; we praise; out of the corner of the eye."

The interior of the château de La Chevrette was not less splendid than the outside. It contained a chapel where the good abbé Martin officiated, as well as the theatre where Francueil had assembled his famous company. Diderot has left a vivid picture of the salon and its occupants, sketched at the time of Madame d'Épinay's return.

We were then in that gloomy and magnificent salon, and we made, diversely occupied, a very agree-

able picture. Toward the window which opens upon
the gardens, M. Grimm was being painted, while Madame d' Épinay leaned upon the back of the chair of
the person who was painting him. A draughtsman
farther away was drawing his profile in crayon. . . .
M. de Saint-Lambert was reading in a corner the
last brochure that I sent you. I was playing chess
with Madame d' Houdetot. The old and good Madame d' Esclavelles, mother of Madame d'Épinay, had
all the little ones around her and was talking with
them and with their tutor. Two sisters of the person
who was painting my friend were embroidering, one
held her ink by hand, and the other used a frame. And
a third was trying a piece of Scarlatti on the clavecin.[1]

On terms of intimacy with Diderot and
the d' Holbachs, under the intellectual influence of Voltaire, dominated by the forceful
personality of Grimm, Madame d' Épinay
was now fully identified with the philosophical party, and her salon increased in
numbers and importance until it included
not only the *encyclopédistes* but the foreign
group, and became the political centre of
the philosophical movement. For not only
the circle which surrounded Madame
d' Épinay was altered and enlarged, but
society in general had lately undergone a

[1] Diderot to Mademoiselle Volland, Sept. 15, 1760.

change, of which she was an example. Her
early life, as was common to the early reign
of Louis XV., had been given to pleasure, but
now, like her own inclinations, the national
life had grown serious; grave thoughts
filled all minds and anxious questions regarding the welfare of society at large were
the singular topics on the lips of every pretty
woman, mingled with arguments on the
rival merits of Gluck or Piccinni; everywhere
the ideas of the philosophers had spread and
were gaining ground. Diderot, the centre of
this movement, was now closely associated
with Madame d' Épinay.

The beauty of moderation in this epoch of
agitation, contradiction, struggle, and aspiration was unknown to Diderot, and his intense nature found vent in his transports of
enthusiasm, in his outbursts of rage, in his
love, devotion, prejudices, in labour, in the
extraordinary vividness of his imagination.
The grace of moderation lies in its absolute
justice and integrity; the enthusiast is seldom
controlled by reason, he is often carried to
excess by his ardent feeling. Diderot,

swayed by his keen emotions, was never complete master of himself; he did not rightly calculate the effect of his writing and, had he lived, would have been as indignant and horror-stricken as Burke at the excesses of the Revolution.   And his friendship, like his former prejudice, for Madame d'Épinay partook of this same character and he who had determined to avoid her became her strongest partisan.   His *Salons,* the most charming of all his works, had their source at La Chevrette.   He had promised Grimm to write something on the pictures which hung in the salon, and he had scarcely returned to Paris when he received a short note from him requesting it immediately.   Surprised and hurt by the somewhat peremptory demand he wrote day and night, and Grimm, "stupefied with admiration," soon received a volume in place of the few lines expected. From this beginning the essays developed which exercised a marked influence on the æsthetic taste of his contemporaries, by pointing out the grace and charm of Boucher, Fragonard, and Chardin; for French artists had then but few admirers among the Parisian amateurs, who saw little beauty in any work but that of the Flemish, Dutch, and Italian schools. Monsieur de Jully, a lover of the arts, and already a collector, profited by Diderot's eloquent pages, and was the first, after Madame Geoffrin, to give practical encouragement to French painting. In 1764 he brought out his *Catalogue Historique du Cabinet de Peintures et de Sculpture Française,* after the manner of Horace Walpole's Strawberry Hill production; it is ornamented with two fine engravings by himself, and is an even more curious and interesting work than Walpole's catalogue.

Madame d'Épinay's circle now included the Marquis de Croismare, the "charming marquis"; Saurin, the poet, who was no sooner introduced than he straightway fell in love; his patron the rich and clever Helvétius, *" qui a dit le secret de tout le monde,"* Madame Du Deffand observed; the agreeable but melancholy Suard, director of the *Gazette Littéraire,* embarrassingly enamoured of the beautiful Baronne d'Holbach as well as of his

THE BARONESS D'HOLBACH.

After a Painting by Varin.

hostess; l' abbé Raynal, the originator of the *Correspondance Littéraire,* which Grimm now directed; Galiani, the *gentil abbé;* and Gatti, the celebrated Florentine physician, introduced by Galiani. All of these shared her pleasure in her correspondence with Voltaire, and as eagerly awaited his letters, for the friendship begun at Geneva was continued by a regular correspondence. Absence had not diminished Voltaire's admiration. "Adieu, my beautiful philosopher," he ends a letter, "you are adored at Délices, you are adored at Paris; you are adored present and absent. Our homage to all those who belong to you, to all those who surround you."

The passion for theatrical representation had now reached its highest point, and performances at private houses vied with the Théâtre Français and the Opéra Comique. Voltaire had decided to have *Tancrède* acted in Paris, and Madame d'Épinay and her friends were in a state of excitement and expectation. All Paris was present at the performance, but they, who were naturally privileged, had places together, and its tremendous ovation was afterward discussed at the supper which followed at Madame d'Épinay's.

The next winter Diderot produced *Le Père de Famille,* at the Théâtre Français. This work ranked with *Tancrède,* and its appearance was a great event. The detestation and fear of the Court for Diderot and his teachings was the topic of the day, and the advent of the piece was awaited with impatience. Tragedies in verse being the received form of plays, and their heroes, as a matter of course, kings and princes, the *Père de Famille,* written in prose, its characters belonging to the bourgeoisie, which aimed at homeliness, broke with all traditions; it was as much a point of departure for the modern drama as was the *Castle of Otranto* for English romance. Diderot's friends, aware of the formidable cabal raised against it, were apprehensive, but the sympathy of the audience was gained from the first. Diderot was too nervous to witness the first performances, but the third night he attended with Madame d'Épinay, and a joyous sup-

per followed at her house, as after *Tancrède,*
and congratulations, compliments, criticism on the staging and the acting, and
hopes and plans for future triumphs ended
the evening.

But all the while Madame d' Épinay's domestic anxieties were steadily increasing.
The wildly extravagant life of Monsieur
d' Épinay had made such inroads in their
income that they were obliged to leave La
Chevrette for their smaller property of La
Briche, which soon, also, had to be given up.
The town house was gone, and necessity
drove her from one quarter of Paris to another. Destitution stared her in the face.
And beside the ills of poverty she was forced
to suffer a greater misfortune ; disappointment in her son came to crown her sorrows,
for in spite of her careful education, he developed more and more the unfortunate pre-
dilections of his father. The means taken to
protect themselves against his prodigality
seems curious to us, but it is an excellent
illustration of the unlimited control which
parents had over their children before the

Revolution. Utterly unable to restrain him in his downward career, or to pay his debts, a *lettre de cachet* was asked for and obtained under which he was imprisoned ; liberated in two years'time, he again contracted debts, when his parents protected themselves by depriving him of his civil rights ; finally he was exiled from France. Madame d'Épinay was more fortunate in her daughter who, brought up in the faith of her pious grandmother, clung to her belief throughout that period when the most religious were scarcely deists. At fifteen she was happily married to the Vicomte de Belzunce and her mother rejoiced that the *douce vicomtesse* should be comfortably established and out of reach of her father.

As worldly prosperity declined, the reputation of Madame d'Épinay became more wide-spread and attained its greatest celebrity. Any evening might be seen in her salon the Comte de Fuentès, Spanish Ambassador, and his sons, Prince Pignatelli and the Marquis de Mora, the latter celebrated for his connection with Julie de Lespinasse—all

three friends of Galiani ; the Marquis Caraccioli, also intimate with Galiani ; the Baron
de Gleichen of Denmark, one of Madame Du
Deffand's circle, and desperately in love
with her friend, the charming Duchesse de
Choiseul ; and the Comte de Creutz, afterward first minister to Gustavus III. Lord
Stormont, the English Ambassador, did not
arrive in Paris until after Galiani's recall,
but he had so high an opinion of him that
when discussion grew high he would invariably suggest that Galiani should be chosen
as judge. In 1767, Rousseau, half distracted,
embroiled with Hume, returned from his unhappy visit to England and appeared again
in Paris ; the reading from the *Confessions*
which followed was far from agreeable either
to Madame d' Épinay or to Grimm and she
succeeded in having it interdicted as libel.

In the opening summer of 1769, abbé Galiani, his recall demanded by the Duc de Choiseul, left Paris. It was a great deprivation
to Madame d' Épinay and her salon, to all
of whom he was the *cher abbé* while for him
it was an intellectual exile which he never

ceased to bewail. "I am always inconsolable to have left Paris," he wrote ;" it does not concern my pleasure only, it concerns my life ; I feel and I prove every day more that it is physically impossible for me to live outside Paris. Mourn me for dead if I do not return." [1]

By long and intimate letters the two friends attempted to bridge over the separating distance, and their correspondence, which lasted till her death, was henceforth a great resource to him and helpful to her, for, beside the power of eloquence, he possessed that more human force, the gift of sympathy; and though his letters lack something of the gaiety which Paris and congenial companions had inspired, they, like his conversation, are intuitive, spontaneous, and full ot wit, humour, and imagination. Madame d'Épinay admired his mind, appreciated his kind heart, and enjoyed his good spirits. From the beginning of their friendship she wished the public to have the benefit of his ideas, and urged him to publish them.

[1] *Lettres de l'Abbé Galiani à Madame d' Épinay,* t. i., p. 7.

He depended much on her judgment
and practical help. "I wish," he wrote,
in 1765, "to retouch the style and the
scenes. . . . Ennoble the rôle of the con-
sul, make the valet funny, the *précieuse*
ridiculous ; that is what I ask of you. Some
scenes should be lengthened. If you do not
wish to take so much trouble, at least mark
the faults of language, the vulgarities of
style, and that which shocks you most." [1]

Here we find how much the abbé valued
her power of criticism, and he naturally
looked to her for assistance in that time of
trial when his hurried leave prevented him
from bringing out the *Dialogues sur les Blés*.
The celebrated work which was to draw down
such violent invective was barely completed,
and Galiani entrusted it to Diderot and
Madame d'Épinay to revise—a labour by
which the book was much the gainer—and
to see it through the press, no light task in
face of the declared enmity of the Duc de
Choiseul. Grimm, invited to Germany about
the same time, also left with them the con-

[1] *Lettres de l'Abbé Galiani à Madame d'Épinay*, t. i., p. 2.

tinuance of the *Correspondance Littéraire*.

It was not the first time that Madame d'Épinay had helped Grimm in this undertaking. Their collaboration had its beginning in discussions as to material, for these private and personal letters which were sent every fortnight during a period of thirty-seven years to the different courts of Europe, held the place of the literary, artistic, and society journals of to-day; criticism, for which her analytic faculty and her power of observation made her a valuable coadjutor, followed, and by 1762 they had begun systematic work together. Literary labour was not new to Madame d'Épinay. Her early letters, written for the instruction of her son, were put into form and printed when she was in Geneva, with her *Portrait* of Madame d'Houdetot, under the title *Lettres et Portrait*. The atmosphere of the period was so critical that Madame d'Épinay was obliged to criticise herself, and it is with an ingenuous and engaging candour which not only attracts us by its naïve self-revelation of the personality of a woman who has been dead for a century and a half, but explains the charm which was felt by every one who entered her house. Yet Madame d'Épinay, like other leading French women of the eighteenth century, though intimate with men of letters and possessing literary capacity, never seriously attempted to rival them in their own field ; she was satisfied to be supreme in her salon. For if we glance critically at what she wrote we shall find that *Mes Moments Heureux* is but a collection of letters, personal sketches, and a few verses which, however interesting from the point of view of character, it would be exaggeration to regard as a serious literary study; not that it lacks many of the qualities which are most delightful in a book, but they are such as are found in the spontaneous form of correspondence or diaries. *L'Amitié de Deux Jolies Femmes* and *Un Rêve de Mademoiselle Clairon* were never published in her lifetime, and are mere trifles. The *Conversations d'Émilie,* on her favourite educational theme, and which brought her unexpected fame, can scarcely be called a literary work nor would it now excite much interest; it was but advice such as any reasonable and careful mother would impart to her child ; but it is for this very reason that it is so remarkable, for it was a sign of moral revolution, of the rebellion of thoughtful women against habits and customs from which no one had suffered more than Madame d'Épinay herself. Appearing early in January of 1775, it immediately excited a wide-spread interest and passed through many editions. All her friends hastened to express their appreciation and delight, and Catherine II, to whom the second edition was dedicated, adopted her methods in the education of her grandson. Madame d'Épinay stood in sore need of these evidences of the friendship upon which she had all her life so much depended. Grimm was now almost constantly abroad, Diderot had joined him, and while they were enjoying St. Petersburg and the attentions of the Empress, Madame d'Épinay, now a confirmed invalid, suffering, sad, grew daily more feeble, and so desperate was her pecuniary state that, had it not been for a pension from Catherine, by which the Empress marked

DIDEROT.
From an Old Painting.

her appreciation of the author of *Les Convers-ations d'Émilie,* she would have been in actual want.

For a little time Voltaire's dramatic return to Paris in 1778 cheered her; to a letter ap-prising Galiani of the great event, he replied, "Your two letters of the 1st and 22d of March have given me infinite pleasure, and have diminished my regret not to be in Paris to see the phenomenon of Voltaire. You paint it in such vivid colours that I see it and hear it, and I laugh most heartily."[1] To Madame d'Épinay's delight Voltaire had taken quarters near her, but her joy was soon turned to mourning; the excitement of the continuous demonstrations culminating in the apotheosis at the Théâtre Français was too great for Voltaire's strength. He died May 30th, and the public idol was refused a grave in the city which had wor-shipped him.

In 1783 *Les Conversations d'Émilie* was crowned by the French Academy and given

[1] *Lettres de l'Abbé Galiani á Madame d'Épinay,* t. ii., p. 315.

the prize of utility founded by Monthyon
and then presented for the first time. Saint-
Lambert was chosen to announce it to her.
Three months later, at the age of fifty-
seven, she died.

VIII

The biographers of Madame d'Épinay and
the editors of the *Mémoires* assert that they
were never meant for publication. No doubt
this was true of the original manuscript,
but changes and interpolations recently
discovered in this manuscript in the handwriting of Grimm, and in which Diderot
is also implicated, dispute past views on
this point.[1] The *Memoires,* at any rate,
did not reach the public before 1818, when
the book ran through three editions in six
months, and when the sensation incident
to its personal features had subsided it
was—and has remained—still in demand.
Though not always correct in detail, yet,
more perfectly, probably, than any other

---

[1] See *Jean Jacques Rousseau*, by Frederika Macdonald, London,
Chapman & Hall, New York, G. P. Putnam's Sons, 1906.

work, it gives us a picture of the intellectual
society of France in the middle and last half
of the century. Madame d'Épinay was forty
when she conceived the idea of writing
down the story of her life; the form of a
romance was necessary out of regard for
the well-known people about her, but, if
their names were changed, their sentiments,
sayings, and doings belonged literally to
that society of which she was a centre.
In her story we have a complete record of a
woman of the world of the eighteenth century and by its pitiless light we are able to
understand some of the causes which led
to the Revolution. Madame d'Épinay had
a philosophical order of mind and, if this interdicted imagination, we are the gainers in
these *Mémoires,* knowing them to give exact
types of the period. The slight veil demanded to save susceptibilities discarded,
we are in the midst of a world which vividly
lives, even though it is a world of sensation
and of ideas rather than of events. Her salon
was the pivot about which circled the greatest mental activity; it was filled with think-

ers whose minds were bent on untangling the knotty problems of their age; it was the salon which gave the greatest impetus to the philosophical movement.

Madame d'Épinay's work shows the preponderating influence of Rousseau and her writings possess features in common with those of the philosopher. Education is the absorbing subject of thought with each; in the *Mémoires* and *Confessions* we are living in the same period, and among the same people; the same philosophy is preached, and the authors vie with each other in their frankness and in their extraordinarily lifelike pictures of the remarkable epoch in which they lived.

Though so closely connected with the avowed enemies of the Church, Madame d'Épinay was essentially religious. Her children were reared in strict observance of their religious duties and moral obligations; together they visited the poor and the sick, when she encouraged their natural sympathy with distress, and pointed out their connection with humanity in its different forms.

We see the practical application of her philosophical ideas when Madame d' Épinay introduced her son to business, which she wished him to learn from the foundation, and which she regarded from an absolutely unbiassed and modern point of view. He did not share her opinions, but his complaints were met by sound advice:

I cannot pity you much for being obliged to bring the candles, to sweep the office, because all that is not very grievous; it is only a prejudiced dunce who could attach humiliation to that, and do not be deceived; if there is a real distance between the profession of the merchant and the place of a farmer general, it is all to the advantage of the merchant; for observe that he lives and grows rich by the work of his brain and of his genius, and the other becomes rich by impositions upon the individual, . . . my project . . . is not to leave you in commerce, not that I disdain that career for you, but, on the contrary, because you have not enough talent to distinguish yourself there. [1]

Madame d' Épinay, though considerably younger, survived Madame Du Deffand only three years. Each to the last held a brilliant court of her own in the same city at a time

[1] *Derniéres Années de Madame d' Épinay,* par Lucien Péney et Gaston Maugras, Paris, Calmann Lé.y, 1894, p. 295.

when intellect alone had power to place a woman at the head of society. No two persons could have been more opposite in temperament, but each seized the one career open to the ambition of a woman of her rank in the eighteenth century — a social supremacy over a group of remarkable friends and associates. Through years of ill-health Madame d' Épinay, her children absent, her friends separated, remained courageous and interested in the world about her, preserving her charm to the last, broadening in mind and disposition as the years went by, and amply redeeming the mistakes of youth, —" She may err, but she will never be irredeemably lost,"—mistakes inseparable from an education and from a state of society of which she was at once a victim and a type.

JULIE DE LESPINASSE

JULIE DE LESPINASSE

1732.   Born.

1752.   Death of the Comtesse d' Albon.

1752.   Meeting with the Marquise Du Deffand. Leaves
the château de Champrond.

1754.   Arrives at convent of St. Joseph in Paris.
Friendship formed with d' Alembert.

1764.   Rupture with Madame Du Deffand.   Opening
of her own salon.

1766.   Meeting with the Marquis de Mora.

1772.   Mora leaves Paris for the last time and Julie
meets the Comte de Guibert.

1774.   Death of Mora.

1776.   Death.

JULIE DE LESPINASSE

I

STUDIES have been presented of Madame
Du Deffand and of Madame d'Épinay,
each of whom, as I have pointed out, was not
only personally attractive, but was a type of
the women of the eighteenth century. In-
tuitively perceptive of, and keenly sensible
to, the influences at work about them, they
—as well as more seemingly dangerous mal-
contents—were rising in revolt against usages
antagonistic to the well-being of the Frenchwoman. Unaware of the precarious nature
of its existence, they were the ornaments
and the victims of that glittering, superficial society, the personal charm of which
has never been equalled.

In the preceding pages I have endeavoured
to illustrate the forces by which the gatherings known as the salons were affected, and
to show the characteristics of the women

with whom they are in our minds associated. Julie de Lespinasse, it may be, is less of a representative figure, but she best illustrates the struggle between individuality and convention, and among all the women who have attained celebrity in any age she stands forth, beside the Greek Sappho, a pre-eminent example of the emotional type.

Those remarkable women who held salons were not generally distinguished for their happy lives, but it was especially the fate of Julie de Lespinasse to be unhappy, and we feel an exceeding pity as we follow the life of one born under a cloud and pursued by misfortune. By the publication of her letters she is seen in a clearer light by succeeding generations than she was by her contemporaries, from whom, with one or two exceptions, her highly strung, deeply emotional temperament was concealed. She hid her feelings so well that she succeeded in deceiving her most intimate friends, who saw in her only the clever, charming, sympathetic companion and confidante. They scarcely realised — though warned by her

D'ALEMBERT.

After the Painting, by Chardin.

Reproduced by permission of Brown, Clement & Company.

frail appearance — her precarious hold on life, and still less suspected the struggles of an intense nature between a past and present passion. It was long after her death before its intricacies and depths were revealed by her letters in their extraordinary avowals of regret and remorse and of strangely intermingled exaltation and pain.

II

Julie de Lespinasse was born at Lyons, November 9, 1732. She was the daughter of the Comtesse d' Albon, who at the time of her birth had been living for some years apart from her husband. The Countess belonged to an old and noble family, and was very rich, the child receiving the name of Lespinasse from a part of her large property, while Julie was her own name. Julie's father, in the gossip of the time, was said to be the Cardinal de Tencin, but it has now been established that he was the Comte de Vichy, Madame Du Deffand's eldest brother, and who, seven years after Julie's birth, had married Madame d' Albon's eldest daughter, a condition of affairs which explains certain veiled yet marked allusions to Julie's history which are found in her letters.

" My history is a compound of circumstances, so calamitous, so horrible," she wrote, "that it proves that the truth is often incredible."[1] And also : " I who have experienced only *atrocities* from the persons from whom I ought to expect solace !"[2]

Her childhood and early youth must, however, have been happy enough—though La Harpe tells a dramatic tale of the cloister and of danger from poison—for it was really passed with her mother in the ancient château d' Avauges, in the romantic country between Lyons and Tartare. She was educated better than was usual and was plainly the Countess's favourite. But at sixteen a great misfortune befell her in the loss of her mother, who, dying suddenly, was unable to complete the arrangements

[1] *Correspondance entre Mademoiselle de Lespinasse et le Comte de Guibert*, par le Comte de Villeneuve-Guibert, Paris, Calmann Lévy, 1906, p. 127.
[2] *Lettres Inédites de Mademoiselle de Lespinasse,* publiées par M. Charles Henry, Paris, E. Dentu, 1887, p. 109.

she had contemplated for Julie's settlement, leaving her by will only three hundred livres in rente viagère, the smallness of the amount to be accounted for, probably, by the delicacy of their relations. On her deathbed the Countess attempted to supplement the bequest by giving her secretly a sum of ready money which would make her virtually independent, and put in her hands the key to the cabinet which contained it. But the girl showed her confiding nature and her disinterestedness by delivering the key to her brother, who thereupon took the cabinet and its contents for himself. Though this act might have reassured them, the family were continually tormented with the fear that Julie would claim her birthright, for as she was born after marriage, she was, by law, entitled to share in their inheritance, and from this time she was exposed to their merciless jealousy.

They did not dare lose sight of her lest, out of their watchful supervision, she should claim her rights and bring action against them. Julie was now, therefore, installed at the château de Champrond, where she was given the post of governess to her sister's children, and where her services soon became invaluable to the entire family. The unfortunate circumstances of her birth were now generally recognised and her position from a favourite child became that of a poor and despised dependent. Such an existence, amid such surroundings, was not to be supported and, after two years of uncomplaining silence, she made up her mind to enter a convent, though it was not until a year later that she signified this intention to her sister, the Comtesse de Vichy, who momentarily turned her from such a course. The following year, however, a powerful friend came to her rescue.

III

It is the brilliant, masterful Marquise Du Deffand who now enters into the story of Julie's life. The Comte de Vichy—as has been previously told—was Madame Du Deffand's brother, and these two women, destined to have so important an influence on

each other's lives, were connected by blood.
Madame Du Deffand was now fifty-five, and
threatened with total blindness. She came
to Champrond toward the end of the summer of 1752, with the half formed purpose
of spending her remaining days with her
kindred, and here she met Julie and saw
that, if not pretty, she had a charming manner and a graceful, even distinguished appearance. She perceived, too, that the
young girl was indispensable in the family,
yet was unloved, uncared for, and housed
only on sufferance. With her usual quick
insight the visitor at once appreciated the
circumstances, and seized her opportunity.
Now convinced that she could neither give
up Paris nor become a provincial and realising the benefit such a companion might be
to her in her growing infirmity, Julie was
invited to join her in a common life in Paris.
The obligations and requirements the position would entail were, however, plainly
pointed out, and Julie was especially advised
what she should avoid. Those warnings
relating to Madame Du Deffand's friends,

and particularly to d' Alembert, when read in the light of later events, seem prophetic of impending disaster.

It was on April 8, 1754, that Julie received the last of many letters from Madame Du Deffand before the final step was taken. Many jealousies, many suspicions, had to be quieted before the consent of the family could be gained, but her mission had been successfully concluded, though Julie was advised of the expediency of secrecy.

There remains nothing more but to speak to you of the joy I shall have to see you and to live with you. I am going to write at once to the Cardinal to beg him to arrange to send you as soon as he possibly can. Do not let your plans be known until the very day of your departure; . . . Adieu, my queen, make your preparations; and come to be the happiness and the consolation of my life.[1]

Before her final release, however, many negotiations were, in that age of family authority, necessary, and these cost Madame Du Deffand some trouble. But the support of the Queen, Marie Leczinska, was

[1] *Lettres de Mademoiselle de Lespinasse*, par Eugéne Asse, Paris, Bibliothéque Charpentier, 1876, p. lxxix.

obtained, and, after an interval of eighteen
months, which Julie passed in a convent at
Lyons, the sanction of the Comte de Vichy
was secured and she was permitted to join
Madame Du Deffand, though she was
henceforth left entirely dependent on her
generosity. That very month the Cardinal
de Tencin saw Julie depart in the diligence
to Paris.

Julie had now undertaken to be a companion to an elderly woman who was a
victim of insomnia, and was rapidly becoming blind. Such a position was not easy
to fill, and her life at this time is generally
supposed to have been a time of trial, but
the character and circumstances of both
women were such that they lived together
for ten years in a connection which was
probably in the interest of each.

Julie was affectionately received at the
convent of St. Joseph, in the rue St.-Domi-
nique, to which Madame Du Deffand had
returned, occupying again her old rooms
and her famous tonneau. With her innate
love of justice Madame Du Deffand could

not be without a keen sense of responsi-
bility toward her young companion, and
we see them enter into their new relations
bound together by hope on one side and
gratitude on the other and by a feeling of
mutual dependence.

The life of Julie de Lespinasse naturally di-
vides itself into three parts. With the first
of these, her childhood and her early womanhood, passed in seclusion, we have done
when she entered the service of Madame
Du Deffand. The two subsequent periods
are those which have made her celebrated.
The ten years during which she lived with
Madame Du Deffand, whatever may have
been her influence over the friends of her
protectress, and however much her tact,
ability, and charm were creating friends for
herself, she was a dependent, and a dependent only. But from 1764 to her death, in
1776, she is what Madame Du Deffand affectionately called her in her early letters, a
queen—*ma reine,*—for she ruled over a circle
as brilliant and numerous as any in Paris
with an unequalled social power. "In

truth"—she is writing to Monsieur de Guibert—"I had a great success"—she had
seen many people in the day,—"because I
brought out the charm and the wit (*esprit*)
of the persons with whom I was."[1] To
know one's powers is to possess the secret
of success, and Julie de Lespinasse understood her own capacity. "Mon ami, I know
myself so well that I am tempted to think
you are mocking me when you speak of my
successes in society. . . . It is eight
years since I retired from the world." She
is writing in 1774, only two years before her
death, when her health was already broken.
"From the moment that I loved I felt a disgust for such successes."[2] This self-know-
ledge and this abnormal capacity for social
success were the effects of an unusual sensitiveness of temperament, increased by an
unnatural youth and by her service with
Madame Du Deffand. Julie de Lespinasse,
as she was known to Marmontel and d' Alem-

[1] *Correspondance entre Mademoiselle de Lespinasse et le Comte
de Guibert,* par le Comte de Villeneuve-Guibert, Paris, Calmann
Levy, 1906., p. 188.

[2] *Ibid.*

bert and the leaders of intellectual life in
Paris at the beginning of the last half of the
eighteenth century, was a being resulting
from a remarkable character placed from
youth in an environment which was suited
to the development of singularities of mind
and temperament. But I have digressed
somewhat from the story of her life, which
must be briefly sketched in the salon of
Madame Du Deffand and in her own famous
salon.

I will announce your arrival to no one, I will tell
the people who first see you that you are a young girl
from my province who wishes to enter a convent and
that I have offered you a home until you have found
the one you like. I will treat you not only with politeness but with consideration, in order that you may
be received with due respect ; I will confide my real
intentions to a very small number of friends and after
the space of three, four, or five months we will know
how to accommodate ourselves to each other and
then we shall be able to conduct ourselves with less
reserve. [1]

The promises which this letter, written
February 13, 1754, contained were conscien-

[1] *Lettres de Mademoiselle de Lespinasse*, par Eugène Asse, 1876,
p. lxxi, Bibliothèque Charpentier.

tiously fulfilled and Julie not only proved an invaluable companion to Madame Du Deffand, who freely expressed her satisfaction with the success of her project, but she brought a new element into her entire circle ; an element of youth and gaiety, a vivacity and an enthusiasm of fresh impressions which enlivened the *blasé* courtiers and invigorated fatigued intellects.

How feeble are expressions to describe that which one feels strongly! The mind finds words, the soul would have to create a new language. Yes, certainly, I have more sensations than there are words to describe them.[1]

Impossible as was expression to such a temperament, something of its delicacy and also of its intensity was felt by every one, and lent inexpressible interest to every word and look. She fitted easily into her new conditions and while, among unkind relatives and their unresponsive, provincial friends, she had been timid and ill at ease, in the critical and exacting society of the capital she

[1] *Lettres de Mademoiselle de Lespinasse*, par Eugène Asse, Paris, Bibliothèque Charpentier, 1876, p. 75.

found herself quite at home.   The Prince de Beauvau said that she ranked in his esteem with the incomparable Formont, the most charming and the most beloved in this perhaps rather coldly brilliant coterie ; and the accomplished Chevalier d' Aydie, who regarded every woman from the elevated standpoint of Mademoiselle Aissé, was equally appreciative in his judgment.

Mademoiselle is keenly touched by the charming things you say of her ; when you know her better you will see how well she merits them ; every day I am more pleased with her [Madame Du Deffand wrote the Chevalier, to which he replied]:

I am well pleased with the opinion I had of her from the first and I pray you to find some place for me in her good will.

Julie de Lespinasse was a pronounced success.   She realised her debt to the Marquise and appreciated the society to which in an unprecedented degree, considering her experience and circumstances, she had been so freely admitted.   Many years later, in the full tide of popularity and power, and when her own salon rivalled that of the convent of St. Joseph, she wrote:

See what an education I have received: Madame Du Deffand (for she ought to be cited for *esprit*), Président Hénault, Abbé Bon, the Archbishop of Toulouse, the Archbishop of Aix, M. Turgot, M. d' Alembert, Abbé de Boismont, M. de Mora, these are the men who have taught me to speak, to think.[1]

No serious love affairs ruffled the current of her life during this early period, and in this brilliant company her mind rapidly developed. Completely under the spell of such stimulating intellectual pressure, which entirely satisfied her, she felt no need of the excursions into the realm of sentimental adventures or of cultivating the fashionable emotions common to her day. A correspondence with a young Irishman by the name of Taaffe—introduced to the convent of St. Joseph, in 1757, by Crawford, who later performed the same good office for Horace Walpole, another illustration of the international social intercourse of the time—gives some colour to the probably exaggerated reports of the impression the Irishman made on her youthful fancy. Letters from him are still in

[1] *Correspondance de Mademoiselle de Lespinasse et le Comte de Guibert*, par le Comte de Villeneuve-Guibert, Paris, Calmann-Lévy, 1906, p. 167.

existence, declaring his love for Julie, and expressing his gratitude to Madame Du Deffand for the care she had bestowed on her. But as Julie never, in any of the letters in which she so freely divulges the history of her inner life, refers to this episode, it is doubtful if, at this time of her life, she were capable of the strong emotions which, later, consumed her very existence.

But we have approached a signal point in Julie's career. Any connection with Madame Du Deffand made certain, at this time, relations with d'Alembert and he, henceforth, for the greater part, may be said to have influenced her mind, character, and future.

IV

D'Alembert was now the most cherished friend Madame Du Deffand possessed, and a daily visitor. So much younger than herself, her friendship was of a maternal nature and she watched over his career, making use of all her powerful influence in his behalf.

D'Alembert was born in 1717 and was therefore thirty-seven at the time of Julie's advent.   Deserted at his birth, largely self-educated, the miserable foundling had, nevertheless, lifted himself by his attainments and discoveries above his scientific contemporaries. Mathematician, philosopher, and writer, he stood on an intellectual pre-eminence and, from the time of his brilliant work on the *Encyclopédie,* at the head of the philosophical party in Paris.   Add to this, brilliant conversational powers, and a gay disposition, and a social success was assured.   D'Alembert was still a young man, and youth, propinquity, similar tastes, and the bond of a common misfortune[1] inevitably drew Madame Du Deffand's two protégés together.   D'Alembert was already reckoned among the greatest living mathematicians ; admitted to the Academy of Sciences in 1741, he had lately been elected to the French Academy through Madame Du Deffand's efforts, and he was beginning his work, in collaboration with Diderot, on the *Encyclopédie.* Sought after at home and abroad, any one must have been flattered by the regard of such a man, but it

[1] D'Alembert was the illegitimate son of Madame de Tencin and the Chevalier Destouches.

appears that his affection was never so warmly reciprocated as it deserved, though Julie
valued his friendship, and fully realised, too,
what it was worth to her.

A few years passed in tranquillity before
dissensions crept in. Though intellectually
they had much in common, Madame Du
Deffand's more masculine mind was not
in sympathy with the sensitive, intensely
emotional temperament with which Julie
de Lespinasse was endowed to excess, and,
as the older woman's infirmities grew upon
her, and more services were required, her
appreciation lessened, while her companion's early gratitude became lukewarm.
Julie's chief duty was to read aloud at night,
a task which often lasted till day brought a
short period of repose for each and, at last,
following a time of growing coldness and mutual dissatisfaction, their relations were sum-
marily brought to a close by the disclosure
that Julie, taking advantage of Madame Du
Deffand's habit of late rising, was deceitfully
holding a salon of her own, composed of the
choicest spirits of her mistress's following.

In her own chamber, looking out upon the courtyard, the dangerously fascinating companion received d' Alembert, Condorcet, Turgot, and others, the most capable minds of that clever, ultra-refined, and aristocratic society which Madame Du Deffand's ability, wit, and social power had attracted. In this modest apartment was held the beginning of Julie's own salon. For one brief hour it was the scene of the most animated and sparkling conversation. The time was short and therefore the more precious, and each must have realised that these were, in a way, clandestine meetings, that if, or rather when, exposed—for no one could hope that these secret reunions would continue indefinitely without coming to the knowledge of Madame Du Deffand— she must look upon them as treasonable, and upon the visitors as traitors. Thus they had the added zest of the ephemeral and the doubtful. These gatherings were continued, however, several years, and the interval between five and six, the hour before Madame Du Deffand received, came to be eagerly anticipated by both hostess and guests as the best in the day. But the hour had run its course. Madame Du Deffand had for some time looked upon d' Alembert's growing regard for Julie with disfavour, and with reason, since, as his admiration of the younger lady increased, his attentions to the elder diminished. Madame Du Deffand's affection for her favourite was too strong to let her share him with any one, nor could so proud a woman permit a rival in her salon, and all was ripe for trouble when discovery brought matters to a crisis.

It is natural to inquire if Julie's behaviour was due to a fault of character or if justification can be found for her. The answer is that in part, at least, her defection may be laid at the door of her friends ; they admired her, they were fond of her, they tempted her, they participated in her fault. Arbitrary and arrogant, Madame Du Deffand claimed all attentions, and that they might see something of her who had become already, in truth, her rival, it easily came to pass that they arrived, by degrees, earlier until their and her hour became a daily habit. She had bewitched them, not by black arts, but rather by her superiority, and they were carried away by the ardour and susceptibility, the quick responsiveness, of her temperament. Julie de Lespinasse was nervous, sensitive, and impressionable to an extreme degree; viewed psychologically, she possessed the exalted, emotional susceptibility of the psychopathic type. We are informed by Professor William James that : "When a superior intellect and a psychopathic temperament coalesce in the same individual, we have the best possible conditions for the kind of effective genius that gets into biographical dictionaries." [1] Such a being was Julie de Lespinasse.

She was now placed in a difficult position. Practically without resources, one course alone remained to her; but the humble apology that she offered was promptly declined in bitterly reproachful words. In

---

[1] *The Varieties of Religious Experience*, Longmans, Green, and Co., 1902, p. 23.

the first explosion of indignation and anger, bitter words had passed between them which could never be forgotten or forgiven.

I cannot believe that it is a sentiment of friendship which makes you wish to see me [Madame Du Deffand replied to her apologies]; it is impossible to love those who detest and abhor you, by whom one's pride is continually humiliated and broken ; these are your own expressions and the sole impressions which you have received for a long time from those whom you have called your true friends.[1]

The rupture was complete and Julie was turned out of doors. But the friends she had seduced from Madame Du Deffand did not fail at this crisis, and they hurried to her assistance with comforting words and offers of substantial help. The Duchesse de Châtillon proffered her protection, the Maréchale de Luxembourg openly blamed Madame Du Deffand, and suitable apartments for the accommodation of the fugitive were secured in the same convenient neighbourhood of the fashionable quarter of St. Germain, on the rue St. Dominique, opposite the convent of Belle-Chasse. The Maréchale furnished her

[1] *Correspondance Complète de Madame Du Deffand*, ed. M. de Sainte-Aulaire, t. i., p. 291.

rooms and Président Hénault, Turgot, the
Marquis d' Ussé, and Madame de Châtillon
together provided for the first necessaries,
while the Duc de Choiseul, one of Madame
Du Deffand's oldest friends, procured the
new favourite a pension from the King
which, added to other small sums obtained
earlier through the efforts of Madame Du
Deffand, furnished her the wherewithal to
live.

Julie proved herself worthy to be entitled
the rival of Madame Du Deffand, for she succeeded in drawing away her most distinguished friends. Some, such as d' Alembert,
broke the closest ties of years entirely and
for ever, and others could not be prevented
from dividing their allegiance. It was a bitter
portion for the proud Marquise and one won-
ders that she could for a moment tolerate
the presence of those who likewise sought
the salon of her rival. But their numbers
were too numerous. The Comtesse de Boufflers was prominent among those who succeeded in remaining on intimate terms with
both, and Président Hénault, who, though

many years of his life had been bound to that of Madame Du Deffand, was so infatuated with the rising star that, in spite of his advanced years, he proposed marriage, and no pressure from his old friend could ever alter this change of heart. An admirable "portrait" of Julie is to be found in his Mémoires.[1] The Duc and Duchesse de Beauvau, lifelong friends of the older, continued their admiring worship of the younger woman, as did the Chevalier de Chastellux, who afterwards obtained his seat in the Academy through Julie's potent influence. The action of her favourite, the Duchesse de Châtillon, who had rooms at the convent of St. Joseph, added visibly to the chagrin of Madame Du Deffand. "I have not seen her since her grande liaison with la Lespinasse." So contemptuously did she allude to her former companion, the year after Julie's death, when writing to Horace Walpole.

As soon as Walpole came to Paris the

---

[1] *Memoires de President Hénault,* Rec. par le baron de Vigan, Paris, 1855, p. 114.

Marquise excited his animosity—never slow to kindle—against Julie, and thereafter he never lost an opportunity to warn his English friends against her.

I must give you one other caution, without which all would be useless [he wrote General Conway]. There is at Paris a Mademoiselle de Lespinasse, a pretended *bel esprit* who was formerly an humble companion of Madame Du Deffand; and betrayed her and used her very ill. I beg of you not to let anybody carry you thither. It would disoblige my friend of all things in the world, and she would never tell you a syllable; and I own it would hurt me, who have such infinite obligation to her, that I should be very unhappy if a particular friend of mine showed her this disregard. . . . I dwell upon it because she has some enemies so spiteful that they try to carry all English to Mademoiselle de Lespinasse.[1]

But not even the powerful machinery that Madame Du Deffand was able to set in motion could check the flight of the newly arisen aspirant and, from the first, the number of Julie's adherents continually increased. Some of these, as was the case with Madame Geoffrin, Madame Du Deffand would have nothing of. She professed a fine scorn indeed for the entire philosophical party

[1] *Letters of Horace Walpole*, ed. Toynbee, ix., 59.

whose leaders Julie had taken from her, and whom she satirised as "la livrée de Voltaire."

It was natural that Madame Du Deffand, who had torn Walpole from her, should be cordially disliked by Madame Geoffrin, and that she, who had felt Madame Du Deffand's disdain, should be gratified in seeing that pride for once laid low ; she therefore welcomed Julie to the philosophical ranks with much fervour, but the shrewd bourgeoise was personally drawn to Julie, also, through the same irresistible fascination to which all must submit who came under the spell of the " enchantress," and her regard assumed the same practical shape by which she loved to show her interest in her protégés. She sold three precious Van Loos to furnish money for Julie's immediate use, and presented her with a pension of three thousand livres. Julie was the only woman Madame Geoffrin cared to invite to her dinners and, as she grew old and feeble, she depended on her assistance for their continuance.

V

Julie de Lespinasse was thirty-two when, in 1764, she opened her salon in the rue Saint Dominique, and the next eight years form the happy era in her life. Possessed, through the liberality and influence of her friends, of sufficient though modest means, she was now her own mistress, free to take up the manner of life she wished and for which she was so supremely fitted.

Though she is nowhere said to be beautiful, Julie now possessed an even greater personal charm than had first attracted Madame Du Deffand. She was tall and well made, and the grace and dignity of her carriage aroused general attention. To judge from her portrait, her features, though irregular, were pleasing, and her face was illumined by strangely expressive dark eyes whose extreme vivacity indicated something of the intense life within; it was, however, the extreme mobility, the ever varying expression of her countenance which was its chief characteristic and charm. The lack of beauty among the leaders of the salons is striking and, as was almost universally the case, Julie de Lespinasse owed little of her success to any outward attraction. A new misfortune, however, overtook her, for she was no sooner fairly installed in her new quarters than she was seized with the smallpox, the common scourge of her time, from which she did not make a good recovery, for she was not only disfigured, but her sight was impaired and her general health, as well, affected.

D'Alembert, whose unremitting devotion had, perhaps, saved her life, stoutly denied that her appearance was at all injured. "She is somewhat marked," he wrote to Hume, "but without being disfigured the least in the world."

But, like her famous contemporaries, it was the mind of this remarkable woman which compelled attention, and, in addition to her mental gifts, she had been taught the value of self-effacement, and won by it a greater reputation for amiability than can generally be claimed for her rivals. She never troubled people either about her delicate health, her monetary embarrassments, or her sorrows. For a sound foundation in the art of pleasing she was gifted by nature with the wish, to which was added the necessity, of pleasing if she would continue her present mode of life. Such natures invariably practise the tact which Julie de Lespinasse possessed in an infinite degree together with taste, that arbiter of the century, for she was sensitive to the slightest discord in manners or conduct.

Julie could not afford even the modest repasts which her former patroness offered her habitués, but the greater triumph was hers when men and women flocked to her salon in ever increasing numbers. Grimm —who divided the time he could spare from Madame d'Épinay between her and Madame Geoffrin,—with an attempt at humour, makes allusion to her want of beauty and fortune in a letter to the philosophers, whom he addresses as brethren in the philosophical sect:

Sister de Lespinasse wishes it to be known that her circumstances do not permit her to offer either

dinner or supper, and that she has not the least wish
to receive those brethren who would like to come
there for the sake of their stomachs. The Church has
ordered me to say that it is at her disposition, and
that when one has so much mind and merit one can
pass by beauty and fortune. [1]

The warmth of her temperament had its
due effect on Julie de Lespinasse's salon,
awaking the imagination, vivifying topics,
giving life and vigour to the conversation.
No subject was too deep to be undertaken,
no anecdote too slight, if either furnished
instruction or entertainment. Marmontel
gives an account, as an eye-witness, of
her influence over the diversified company
which she and d'Alembert gathered about
them. He likens the dissimilar personalities
grouped in her salon to the chords of an
instrument from which, though diverse in
themselves, she, by her art, drew forth the
most exquisite harmonies. "Nowhere," he
says, "was the conversation more lively,
more brilliant, more solid, or better regulated." The activity of her fancy was

[1] *Grimm, Correspondance Litt.*, 1812, 1813, 1814, 17 tomes, en
3 parties, t. vi., p. 329.

communicated to their minds, but in due
measure. Her imagination was the lever
but it was regulated by her reason and the
minds which she swayed to her liking were
neither feeble in capacity nor wanting in
weight. There were Condillacs and Tur-
gots, and d' Alembert was but a simple,
docile child in her hands. The talent of
the hostess in throwing out a thought for
debate to such men; her own gift for discussion with a precision, sometimes with
an eloquence, like their own; her ingenuity
in introducing new ideas and in varying the
conversation, always with the facility of a
fairy who, by a wave of her wand, changes
at will the scene of her enchantments,—these
talents were not those of any ordinary woman. The trifles of the world and of vanity
could not have interested the same circle
of superior intellects for four hours of each
day.[1]

Emotional and extremely sensitive to impressions, as I have said, Julie de Lespinasse
gave herself freely to her intuitions and

[1] *Mémoires*, Marmontel, t. ii., p. 229.

quick sympathies, creating an enthusiasm which communicated itself to every one. "You make marble feel and matter think," said Guibert.[1] A mental atmosphere peculiar to herself surrounded her, which stimulated and elevated thought, sharpened the perception, and enlarged the intellectual horizon. In this atmosphere each one saw himself at his best and, as in a magic mirror, his ideas, though reflected, were transformed and uplifted. Possessing a genius for friendship, among all those brilliant women who led society she had the largest personal following. She forsook all ordinary pleasures for her salon, receiving every evening from six to ten. So rarely was this rule broken that an occasional visit in the country was an event talked of throughout Paris. She was unique in having no favourite in her salon, for not even d' Alembert was given more prominence than his conversational powers naturally obtained ; undoubtedly his presence was an irresistible magnet but if

[1] " Éloge d'Éliza. *Lettres de Mademoiselle de Lespinasse,* par Eugène Asse , Paris, Bibliothèque Charpentier, p. 359.

MARMONTEL.
From an Old Print.

he attracted men she retained them.[1] A perfect equality reigned, and when the hour
struck any intimates who might have been
on more familiar terms earlier were then
placed on a level with the rest of the
company.

"M. de Marmontel proposed to me to
come last Wednesday and read me his new
comic opera. He came ; there were some
twelve persons present. Behold us in a
circle surrounding him, and listening to the
Vieux Garçon, that was the name of the
piece,"[2] she writes in 1774.

The distinguishing mark of this salon lay
in its variety and in its freedom, which were
its essential features for, naturally following
the lead of Madame Du Deffand, whose
friends had become hers, it retained the
literary and aristocratic elements for which
the salon of Madame Du Deffand was renowned; foreign countries, the court, the
state, the church, and the army, beside the
literary coterie, all having their best repre-

[1] *Correspondance Littéraire,* Grimm, 1812, 1813, 1814, 17 vol.,
t. ix., p. 81.

[2] *Lettres de Mademoiselle de Lespinasse,* par. Eugène Asse,
Paris, Bibliothèque Charpentier, p. 128.

sentatives among her habitués. And also, from her close connection with d'Alembert, the acknowledged philosophical leader, the salon of Julie de Lespinasse was termed philosophical. It was no empty title. That of Madame Geoffrin had a wider, a more public renown, but the freedom of discussion permitted by Julie was in marked contrast to Madame Geoffrin's hard and fast rules, and for this reason the subsidiary salon exercised a greater influence on the philosophical circle than that which was its reputed centre. Seats in the Academy, like reputations, were gained or lost, and public opinion guided, also, to a greater extent in Julie de Lespinasse's salon than in any other. "It was almost a title of consideration to be received in this society," wrote La Harpe.[1]

Julie de Lespinasse was probably the best educated of any of the directors of the salons. She was a linguist, which was particularly useful, enabling her to be agreeable to the strangers who came in great numbers to Paris. She was also well versed in foreign

[1] *Correspondance Littéraire*, La Harpe, 1804, t. 1, p. 386.

literature, as well as in that of her own country, and she delighted especially in the newly arisen English fiction.

As was to be expected, she was one of the most ardent admirers of the genius of Rousseau, though she met him but a few times, and therefore hardly knew him except through his works. Intimacy with Hume might in another have prejudiced the judgment against Rousseau, yet, in spite also of d'Alembert, whose resentment was aroused by being forced into the quarrel, and of repeated warnings from ever-prudent Madame Geoffrin, her sympathies were enlisted for the sensitive, irascible, and perverse philosopher in the furious conflict provoked by Walpole's malicious spirit. Always natural, and instinctively sincere, Julie was out of harmony with the artificial and material mid-century type, and was by nature adapted to appreciate the teachings of Rousseau.

The unique intercourse which existed about the middle of the eighteenth century between some of the first thinkers and men

of letters in England, and the most brilliant
section of French society, is illustrated by the
friendship between Julie de Lespinasse and
David Hume. Hume arrived in Paris as
secretary to Lord Hertford, the newly appointed British Ambassador, on October 14,
1763. The next year came the separation
between Madame Du Deffand and Julie,
which has already been described, and which
absorbed the attention of the fashionable and
intellectual world of Paris. From the moment of his arrival Hume became the fashion,
to the surprise, and perhaps chagrin, of some
of his friends. " He is treated here with a
perfect veneration. His history, so falsified
in many points, so partial in as many, so very
unequal in its parts, is thought the standard
of writing"—so wrote Horace Walpole to
George Montagu in 1765.[1] Lord Charlemont,
who was no better pleased, strikes a more
personal note. " No lady's toilet," he says,
" was complete without Hume's attendance.
At the Opera his broad, unmeaning face was
usually seen *entre deux jolis minois.*" Julie

[1] *Letters of Horace Walpole,* ed. Toynbee. p. 301.

de Lespinasse's rising salon would have lost a singular attraction if Hume had not been one of the frequenters. This is why Madame Du Deffand did not like him; he belonged to the rival salon. "He has displeased me," she wrote, when he was returning to Scotland. "Hating idols I detest their priests and their worshippers." It had been otherwise at first. "The charms and pleasures he has found elsewhere," she wrote, in a melancholy strain, to Crawford, "have taken him away,"[1] and as she had been the first to befriend him, it was not unnatural that his abandonment should be resented. Her old mistress might well regard Julie as a high priestess of Hume, and so the idol was out of favour because she worshipped at its shrine.

If Julie was more discreet than Madame Du Deffand with her tongue, the partisanship of her friends was decided and severe. "As to my neighbour the viper," was the disagreeable way in which d'Alem-

---

[1] *Correspondance Complete de Madame Du Deffand*, M. de Sainte Aulaire, t. 1. p. 48.

bert, in a letter to Hume, begins a reference to his old friend; for Hume and d' Alembert also carried on a correspondence, and the English philosopher proved the esteem in which he held his French colleague, by a legacy of two hundred pounds. The correspondence of Mademoiselle de Lespinasse with Hume throws a good deal of light on the character of this versatile woman. Nothing could be more matter of fact, more unsentimental, than her letters to him, though at the same time they are so unaffected and so friendly that, following upon a sympathetic personal intercourse, they suggest, rather than indicate, the charm which made so many of the ablest and best known men of the age her devoted friends. The friendship of Hume and Julie de Lespinasse illustrates also some of the influences which created the remarkable understanding between the leaders of English and French opinion, the intellectual sympathy, and, on the part of the French, the appreciation, of the freedom which permitted Locke, and at this time Hume, to express, without repression, the most liberal views, whether on religion or politics. The importance of the relations between Hume and Julie de Lespinasse, however, whether as an incident in the history of letters, or as a personal episode, must not be overrated. It cannot for a single moment compare with the famous friendship of Horace Walpole and Madame Du Deffand, each of whom, too, was a fastidious aristocrat as well as a lover of letters, and of intellectual brilliancy. Neither can Hume and Walpole well be compared, and Julie de Lespinasse who was continually sustained by first one and then the other of the two most influential women in Paris, was lifted into a place among the women of the salons. Nor, between Hume and Julie, was there any of that delicate, appreciative, and tender attachment which has given to the relations of Madame Du Deffand and Walpole something of the ideal. But this friendship and others not unlike it have made the eighteenth century memorable, in that a group of men and women met on terms of open and acknowledged intellectual equality. D' Alembert, Diderot, Grimm, Hume, and

Walpole would have been the first to admit that the delightful women in whose salons they were received had as able heads as themselves.

Julie de Lespinasse was a great admirer of the English, as well as of English literature. Sterne was her favourite author, and she made the reputation of the *Sentimental Journey* in Paris by a good translation.[1] She wrote a piece[2] in admirable imitation of Sterne's style which, oddly enough, was first published in England, not appearing in Paris till two years later in a French translation. Richardson was at this time at the height of his popularity, and she was one of those who most appreciated his genius.

VI

The names of Madame Du Deffand and d' Alembert are indissolubly linked with that of Julie de Lespinasse, and she is equally well known as the rival of one and the friend of the other ; we must now, therefore, more

[1] Published in London in 1767.
[2] *Suite du Voyage Sentimental.*

closely consider her connection with d'Alembert.   It was Julie who was the cause of his
obstinacy when he refused the Presidency
of the Academy of Berlin, and also when he
persistently declined to leave Paris for the
Russian capital, notwithstanding the mu-
nificent offers of Catherine II, for from the
time of her rupture with Madame Du Deffand, d' Alembert devoted his life to Julie.
But it cannot be said that, beside her companionship, he received no equivalent, for
her salon served to propagate his philosophical ideas, and guaranteed that honour of
which he was most proud and most jealous
—his place, unquestioned after Voltaire's
death, at the head of the philosophical party,
whose leadership was his chief concern.
The *Portrait* [1] which he addressed to Julie,
in 1777, is a splendid gift—an offering expressing the lofty sentiments which she
had inspired—from one of the first men of
his times to his best friend, for Julie was
always that, as he was hers, though

[1] *Lettres de Mademoiselle de Lespinasse*, par Eugène Asse,
Paris, Bibliothèque Charpentier, 1877, p. 343.

she wandered far from his singleness of attachment.

Julie de Lespinasse's life was remarkably free from ill-natured gossip, and for no woman who occupied such a conspicuous place in society was less of malice shown. Whether it was the general light behaviour of the period, or the respect in which she and d' Alembert were held, that shielded them, at any rate they escaped unpleasant remark, and their intimate association was accepted by society as quite correct. Hume, however, was not, at first, so charitable, not easily believing that simple friendship could be the basis of their relations and, in a letter to England, he plainly puts his own interpretation on the affair. " Since I wrote the above, I went to see Mademoiselle de Lespinasse, d' Alembert's mistress, who is really one of the most sensible women of Paris. "[1] This opinion of her, nevertheless, did not prevent him from immediately opening the cordial relations which were continued for

---

[1] *Life and Correspondence of David Hume*, by J. Hill Burton, London, 1846, vol. ii., p. 237.

so many years by their correspondence.
Her reputation rather gained than suffered
when d'Alembert took up his abode in the
same house for, the year following her estab-
lishment in the rue Saint Dominique, d'Alembert falling ill, she nursed him tenderly and,
as soon as he was able, had him removed
thither, where he lodged for the rest of
her life. A report that they were to be
married was circulated in the gazettes and
d'Alembert unjustifiably denounced Madame Du Deffand as its probable author in an
angry letter to Voltaire :

The person to whom they marry me [in the ga-
zettes] is in truth respected for her high character and
well fitted by her sweet disposition, gentleness, and by
the pleasure which her society gives, to make a husband happy; but she is worthy of a better establishment than mine, and there is neither marriage nor
love between us, but reciprocal esteem and all the
sweetness of friendship. I live actually in the same
house as she, where there are beside ten other
lodgers; this is what has occasioned the talk which
has been going about. I do not doubt besides [he
concludes] but that it has been assisted by Madame
Du Deffand.[1]

[1] March 3, 1766. *Œuvres d' Alembert*, Paris, Berlin, 1822,
t. v., p. 148.

The society of the salon, in the last half of the eighteenth century, worshipped pure intellect.   Birth had lost its prerogative; beauty its sovereignty. The reign of the intellect was supreme even when encumbered with age, infirmity, and ugliness, or handicapped by mean parentage or poverty— a triumph of mind over matter. As I have said hardly one of those women whose influence was paramount in the salons was beautiful, and physical attraction among men was of little account. Neither Julie de Lespinasse nor d'Alembert had or needed personal beauty to make them the most sought after couple in Paris. Yet primal instincts could not be permanently suppressed and Julie, though no one was more inclined for the society of men of intellect, at length surrendered her heart to the charm of youth and a handsome person. It may be that d'Alembert's small stature did not fulfil a romantic ideal and that his high-pitched voice grated on her sensitive nerves, even though, beside his intellectual pre-eminence, his reputation for delicate wit

and scathing satire and his gift for caricature
and story-telling made him easily the first
at any gathering of *bels esprits;* while his
modesty, simplicity, and plainness of manners, his gentle spirit and compassionate
heart, and his regular life, which was in such
contrast to the age, if it brought forth contempt and pity rather than admiration and
esteem, still created a deep impression amid
the follies, the restlessness, and the reckless-
ness which marked it.

His devotion to Julie knew no bounds.
No service was too small to be undertaken
for her; he fetched and carried, and even
ran to the post that she might receive early
tidings from his rivals. The first years which
they spent at the rue Saint Dominique
were a period of unclouded happiness for
both. D'Alembert held the first place in
Julie's affections and there was certainly
some warmth in her sentiments for she once
told him that she was frightened at the
happiness he gave her.[1]

[1] *Lettres de Mademoiselle de Lespinasse*, par Eugène Asse,
Paris, Bibliothèque Charpentier, 1876, p. 374.

VII

Julie de Lespinasse, as so involuntarily, but so clearly, revealed in her now famous letters, will always remain an enthralling subject for those who are interested in the analysis of the human heart. But the story of a temperament at once brilliant and emotional, however fascinating, lies outside the scope of these studies, which are primarily concerned with the relation of certain individualities to the evolution of the society of their epoch. The love of Mora, and the fainter but, for Julie, fatal affection of Guibert—episodes apart so far as regards the progress of French society as seen in the salons,—reveal, however, some of the causes of the irresistible attraction, sometimes destructive of old and long friendships, felt by the most widely different persons for one who was attractive by reason of the subtle qualities of womanhood which always charm men, and of a mind at once vivid, intelligent, and sympathetic, whose influence was admitted by the first philosophers of the age.

In the year 1766 a new figure had appeared upon the scene. The Marquis de Mora, twelve years younger than Julie, was the eldest son of the Comte de Fuentès, the Spanish Ambassador to France. Of great promise, he was declared by d' Alembert to be the most perfect character he had ever known. Much was hoped from him politically by the reform party in France as in Spain. L'abbé Galiani termed him "the first grandee among the grandees of Spain." He was idolised by society, and Julie, meeting the hero of the hour, surrendered to his charm and fell in love. Ministered to with unceasing solicitude by d' Alembert, Julie had enjoyed at once peace and independence ; now, adored by the man who had won her heart, the full tide of life set in, and her deeply passionate nature was fully aroused.

It appears certain that they were engaged to be married. The Marquis's family, however, had other designs for his future ; his delicate health was another anxiety ; Julie therefore concealed their relations and her feelings from her friends, and even from

d' Alembert, who wrote at this very time:
" passion is not in you."

In August of 1772, Mora was obliged by
ill health to leave Paris; the time of his return was uncertain, and Julie was so affected
by the parting that, in the endeavour to
turn her attention from her trouble, she
threw herself with all her natural impetu-
osity, before the month was out, into an
intimacy with a young officer, the Comte
de Guibert, a newcomer in Paris, but already a prominent figure in the army and in
society, and she found herself, before she
was aware of it, under the domination of
a passion from which she unceasingly attempted, but in vain, to escape. "Sorrow,"
she writes, " was the emotion that drew
me to you"; but if her love for Mora was
an idyl, that for Guibert was a tragedy,
and d' Alembert, prophesying the empire a
man such as Guibert might gain over her,
now reads as if inspired. Writing in 1771,
before she had met Guibert, d' Alembert
draws a picture to which the man—and
this time the object of her affections was

eleven years her junior—who obtained such an ascendancy bears a remarkable likeness.

The only thing for which you can be reproached [he wrote,] is your extreme sensitiveness to what is called "good style" in manners and speech; the lack of that quality you think scarcely effaced by the truest sentiment that can be offered you. There are men, even, in whom the presence of that quality supplies the want of all others; you know them such as they are, weak, selfish, full of airs, incapable of deep and constant feeling, but agreeable and charming, and you have a great inclination to prefer them to your more faithful and more sincere friends; with more care and a few more attentions for you they might eclipse all others in your eyes, and perhaps take the place of all.[1]

But in justice to Julie's judgment it must be added that Guibert fascinated and deceived all her society, which regarded him as a young prodigy who would reform politics and the army, for he wrote on both; he aspired as well to the whole field of literature and to academic honours, which he obtained, but not until after the death of Julie de Lespinasse. To be fair, it would appear that his want of proper consideration

[1] *Lettres of Mademoiselle de Lespinasse*, par Eugène Asse, Paris, Bibliothèque Charpentier, 1876, p. 301.

—it cannot be said that he was wanting in appreciation—for Julie, has led her sympathetic critics to underestimate Guibert's ability. To-day his writings have lost their interest, but they impressed his contemporaries as first-rate. His book on military tactics in which he forestalled, in some degree, later authorities, was considered a notable work at the time. He was asked to read his dramatic pieces before Voltaire and the different celebrated persons he visited in his travels, and one was played with considerable success before the King and Queen at Versailles, and also at Chanteloup, where the Duc de Choiseul was comfortably ensconced in semi-royal state. Madame Necker was warm in her praises of him, and later in his life he was the first of Madame de Staël's preferred admirers. Nor was Guibert wanting in practical qualities and capacity for he was a good soldier, and fought bravely in many engagements.

"Monsieur Guibert seeks glory by every road; to receive applause from armies, theatres, and women is a sure means to immortal-

ity," Frederick II wrote to Voltaire in 1775.
Voltaire addressed one of his satires to Guibert, "who appears to me," he told d'Alembert, "a man full of genius and, what is not
less rare, a very amiable man."[1] Young,
handsome, in the fashion, a great future pre-
sumably before him, it was not strange that
he pleased Julie, though it is a proof of odd
weaknesses in human nature that a woman
of so strong a mind should not better have
been able to control her heart.

But intellect alone could not satisfy Julie
de Lespinasse. On September 1, 1775, the
year before her death, her fragile body already
reduced to a pitiable state by her harassed
mind, she thus wrote concerning the unhappy passion which had brought her to
such a condition.

Despising everything but the happiness of loving
and of being loved, I needed neither strength nor virtue
to bear poverty and to disdain the desires of vanity. I
have enjoyed so much, I have felt so deeply the value
of life, that, were it to begin again, I should wish it
might be under the same conditions. To live and to
suffer, heaven and hell, this is for what I should live,

[1] November 19, 1773.

this is what I should wish to experience, this is the air I should wish to breathe.[1]

Painful experience only strengthened her belief in the virtue of love:

There is but one single thing . . . it is love, for all other things remain without response. Consider ambition, avarice, love of glory even, . . . there is only love, passionate love and doing good, which appear to me to be worth the pain of living![2]

A woman who could write such words had desperate needs and, restrained from childhood, forces as of some primeval, unreasoning creature now captured and mastered the clever, supersensitive, critical leader of an ultra-cultivated society.

Two years had passed by when Julie received news that Mora, whose health in the meantime had not improved, was returning to her. His physical delicacy had prevented the confession which she had determined upon, but a change in her letters was evident and the lover, against medical

[1] *Correspondance entre Mademoiselle de Lespinasse et le Comte de Guibert*, par le Comte de Villeneuve-Guibert, Paris, Calmann Lévy, 1906, p. 303.

[2] *Lettres Inédites de Mademoiselle de Lespinasse à Condorcet*, etc. M. Charles Henry, Paris, E. Dentu, 1887, p. 138.

advice, insisted on returning to Paris, but, stricken by a mortal illness, he died on the way, and remorse for what she considered her infidelity to him, added to grief for his death, which occurred at Bordeaux, May 27, 1774, caused her own.   When the news of his death reached Paris, half distraught, she was only prevented from killing herself by Guibert.   After his marriage in the following year, stung alternately by remorse and jealousy, her health rapidly declined until her death—which occurred May 23, 1776, at the age of forty-four,—while all the time d' Alembert, who tenderly watched over her to the last, was alike ignorant of her wild passion for Guibert as of her ardent love for Mora, and her self-revelation in her letters shows with what marvellous skill and self-control she must for years have acted a part.

D' Alembert survived Julie seven years; grief stricken, they were spent in mourning; no one could rouse him from his melancholy broodings and even his public utterances contained pathetic allusions to the solitude

to which her death condemned him; his
room above the unpretentious apartment
which had been the scene of so many
brilliant gatherings and the home of a powerful political party, was exchanged for the
attic in the Louvre to which his post as perpetual secretary of the Academy entitled
him.   The knowledge of the wasted passion
which her death had brought to light continually weighed upon him.   " Why should
love, made to lighten the ills of life for
others, be the torment and the despair of
yours ? " [1]

The loss of Julie, soon followed by that of
Madame Geoffrin, was, moreover, the signal
for the downfall of the philosophic party; it
had been controlled and held in place in these
salons; its decadence now began.

VIII

An analysis of the mental constitution of
Madame Du Deffand and of Julie de Lespinasse shows that they possessed many

[1] *Aux manes de Mademoiselle de Lespinasse.   Lettres de
Mademoiselle de Lespinasse.* Par Eugène Asse, Paris, Bibliothèque
Charpentier, 1876, p. 375.

strikingly similar features. Exceptionally
organised, remarkable in character as in intellect, beside them Madame d' Épinay
appears wanting in force and Madame Geoffrin commonplace. No affectation, no pretension is ever to be found in either Madame
Du Deffand or Julie. They were both
distinguished for their simplicity; both hated
eloquence. Neither loved nature for itself
alone, they were too intensely subjective
and analytical; it was the active exercise
of the mind which gave them pleasure.
Each constantly aspired towards the ideal
and was as constantly disappointed. Each
was extremely critical, and towards herself
as well as towards others. Each wished
passionately to be loved; Madame Du Deffand's asperity arose from this, for she
could never wholly believe in any one.
Each felt the strain of an intense nature
and Julie did not survive the contending
emotions which resulted from the conflict
between conscience and passion.

Julie de Lespinasse's love of truth was
shown in her literary likings. It was

said by the poet Dorat, and others of his school, that she not only made Academicians, but that she also used her influence against those who failed to please her, and prevented their election. It was easy for those who could not obtain a seat to criticise her influence ; habituated to the best in literature, she naturally turned toward large ideas and great themes. Her judgment was respected, many counted upon her advice, and her discretion was absolute. When political power finally fell into the hands of her friends, Turgot and Malesherbes, she realised that the state of affairs was such that it could not be permanently improved and, as events rapidly unfolded, she foresaw that Turgot, in whose energetic reforms she passionately sympathised, would become a victim of his unselfish devotion, and she complained in her letters of his unceasing toil and praised his determination and tranquillity.

"As for me," she wrote Condorcet, "who have neither his courage nor his virtues, I am filled with sadness and with terror. I

CONDORCET.

From an Engraving by Levachez.

believe what I fear, and I think of the future
only with fright." This was written in
May, 1775. Louis XVI had been on the
throne a year, and though she was soon
deploring his extravagance, these forebodings, which the corn riots evoked, are followed by observations on the young King
which call attention to the hope placed in
him.

He showed, [she said] throughout this affair
much wisdom, kindness, and firmness. Yesterday he
wrote two letters to M. Turgot, which do great honour to his heart and mind. Is it not distressing to see
that with a king who wishes well and a ministry
which has a passion for it, it is evil which is done and
that the great part of the public wish only evil?[1]

Julie, so free in bestowing favours, was
reluctant to ask for them. When Turgot
was taken ill her anxiety was great. "It
is a public calamity!" she exclaimed. She
had no way of reaching him at Versailles.
The Duchesse d'Enville and her son, the
Duc de La Rochefoucauld, were among her
most intimate friends, but she hesitated to

[1] *Lettres Inédites de Mademoiselle de Lespinasse*. M. Charles
Henry, Paris, E. Dentu, 1887, p. 149.

ask for a seat in the coach of the Duchess, who was driving out.

"I have not dared ask for a place of the Duchesse d' Enville," she wrote Condorcet. "I fear more than anything to be a charge or a trouble ; my pleasure will always be sacrificed to this fear." [1]

Condorcet, the philosophical and philanthropical Marquis, her "bon Condorcet," as she half affectionately, half maliciously, called him, who, nevertheless, came first in her friendship after d' Alembert, relied, as well as Turgot, upon her counsel and shared with d' Alembert his post as secretary when she was too ill to write. "They are identified with me ; they are necessary to me, like the air in order to breathe ; they do not trouble my soul, but they fill it," she wrote to Guibert of Condorcet and d' Alembert. She was also deeply attached to Suard, who gained his seat in the Academy through her efforts ; others among her intimates were Devaines, the accom-

[1] *Lettres Inédites de Mademoiselle de Lespinasse.* M. Charles Henry, Paris, E. Dentu, 1887, p. 143

plished and clever financier, who left her a legacy ; the abbés Morellet and Arnaud, the Chevalier de Chastellux, Saint-Lambert, and Madame ᵼd' Houdetot. Julie de Lespinasse well knew all the delicate shades, all the subtleties, and differences, in friendship.

"I believe that I shall miss him very much," she wrote, when Caraccioli—the popular Neapolitan Ambassador,—who was one of her most devoted adherents, was about to leave Paris, "but he makes me feel very distinctly the infinite difference that there is between the pleasure which amuses and that which touches or interests."

Though she fervently admired the English constitution and was one of the first on either side of the Channel to appreciate the English novel, she could not be induced to visit England.

Have I not yet told you that I have been pressed, solicited, to go to re-establish my health at Lord Shelburne's ? Here is a man of intellect ; here is the chief of the opposition ; here is the friend of Sterne ; he adores his works. See if he ought not to have the greatest attraction for me, and if I ought not to be much moved by his kind entreaties. [1]

Lord Shelburne passed the summer and autumn of 1774 in Paris; he constantly sought the society of Julie, who was won by his enthusiastic temperament and public spirit. Unlike most of her reforming friends, who were drawn toward Catherine II by her powerful personality, as well as by her benefits, Julie looked upon the Empress with aversion, as the representative of despotism.

"What will you see there?" she wrote Guibert on his way to St. Petersburg. "You will see that which your soul detests, slavery and tyranny, debasement and insolence."

Julie de Lespinasse was termed the Sappho of her time. And not without cause, for she was the centre of a brilliant circle of intellects and a leader in the philosophical school and, like Sappho, her school dwindled away, bereft of her influence. She was, however,

[1] *Lettres de Mademoiselle de Lespinasse to Guibert*, par Eugène Asse, Paris, Bibliothèque Charpentier, 1876, p. 122.

the intellectual Sappho of the kindlier critics, for though her heart was divided between
two passions in the last years of her life, it
was unwillingly, and her love for Guibert
was chiefly the result of her affection for
Mora ; deprived by absence and then by
death of him, she felt a desperate need of
sympathy and solace, and it was from Guibert that she hoped to receive it. Men and
women of strong feelings do not play at love,
and Julie de Lespinasse was utterly devoid
of coquetry. Passionate in everything yet,
such was the justness, the delicacy, the ex-
quisiteness of her taste, she was always elegant, always refined, always dignified.

Women were just as warm in their admiration of Julie de Lespinasse as men, though
their devotion was often rather tolerated than
returned. The friendship of the Duchesse de
Châtillon rose indeed to a veritable passion
and she never ceased to mourn Julie's early
death. Julie sharply criticised the shallow-
ness of the lives of women in general among
the upper classes, lamenting their love of admiration and the pettiness of their aims, and

she often expressed the opinion that the majority, ruled by vanity and ambition, wished to be preferred, not loved; but, provided they had wit or understanding, women were welcomed in her salon as cordially as men. Julie de Lespinasse could be jealous but she was never selfish. She attracted persons not only to herself, but to each other, when in her company. "We all felt ourselves to be friends when with her," wrote Guibert.[1]

Madame Du Deffand's letters have been ranked with those of Madame de Sévigné, as models; like those of her epistolary rival they are addressed to a wide circle and the letters of both are the products of their periods. Julie de Lespinasse had also a large correspondence, though her literary remains are limited to her letters to Guibert, a few to Condorcet, and some scattered writings. Her correspondence with Guibert, of the most private nature, intended for his eye alone, is entirely free in matter and form, and is the spontaneous expression of an ex-

[1] *Éloges d'Éliza. Lettres de Mademoiselle de Lespinasse*, par Eugène Asse, Paris, Bibliothèque Charpentier, 1876, p. 364.

ceptional mental condition. Vibrating with the fervour and exaltation of an extraordinary passion, they place her among the greatest emotional writers, with Sappho and Héloïse. They never fail in admirable propriety of expression ; no offensive word—so frequent in the writing of the time—mars these brilliant pages, and they are exempt from the stiltedness and artificiality which in general marked the English letter writer. She comes in point of time between Fanny Burney and Jane Austen but, not of one epoch any more than of one place, she owes nothing to, neither is she limited by, her environment ; like all masterpieces, her letters might have been written in any period of history, or in any country, and they are singularly free from the wordy exaggeration which characterises the time in which she lived. There is, no doubt, some monotony about them due to their subjective personal nature, repetitions on the same unhappy theme following each other in harassing reiteration ; disappointed love, unsatisfied longing, remorse, despair. These are the key-

notes of the letters to Guibert. Those to
Condorcet are of a wholly different character.
Here there is no blighting passion but, in its
place, the liveliest expression of a singularly
tender and devoted friendship. Solicitude
for his manners—where she finds plenty to
correct—vies with concern for his health, and
for the health of Turgot concerning which
each felt anxious.

Subjective writing does not offer readers
much fact to build upon, though some allusions now and then disclose fleeting glimpses
of her life—dinners at ambassadors' or at min-
isters', or of d'Alembert with her at Madame
Geoffrin's. Music naturally appealed to such
a temperament, and in the war which was
being waged between the different schools,
it was her instinct for the passionate which
was always her guide, though, too just to
give way to prejudice, she openly expressed
an admiration for Grétry, the rival of
Glück, whom she preferred. "But," she
exclaimed, "how can that which pleases be
compared to that which fills the soul?"

Reflective and clear-sighted, her judgments

pierced beneath the surface. " I take intentions into account as others take actions,"she
wrote. Her contemporaries, from whom her
passionate nature was so largely concealed,
yet realised something of its intensity and
power. " The keenest intelligence, the most
ardent soul, the most inflammable imagination which has existed since Sappho," wrote
Marmontel. " Born with nerves, prodigi-
ously sensible," said Grimm.

Julie de Lespinasse will probably have
greater attraction for the readers of to-day
than any other of the distinguished Frenchwomen of the eighteenth century, for her
letters, with their accent of despair, have
given her a very human interest. They
emphasise the fact that the brilliancy of the
salons hid dissatisfied hearts, and that, as I
have pointed out in other papers, there was,
amidst all the intellectual and social vivacity
of the salons, an undercurrent of endeavour
arousing the women who adorned them to
break with the artificiality, the bonds, and
the forms by which natural and simple development was hindered. The marvellous

social success which Julie de Lespinasse achieved did not satisfy her, it was external only ; her very success seemed to make more necessary a purely human sympathy, and the revelation of herself in her letters adds that touch of nature which makes the whole world kin, and gives the reader that sense of companionship and sympathy which makes her live again who would otherwise be a mere historical figure.

She, it is true, is not so exactly characteristic of the age as gentle Madame d'Épinay, clever Madame Geoffrin, or perhaps autocratic Madame Du Deffand, but she exemplifies more than any other of the leaders of society in eighteenth-century Paris the power which so many women then possessed of attracting and influencing men, for she had neither riches, rank, nor beauty, yet her charm could bend to her will the savant and the gallant ; the devotion of her friends was not limited by age or calling, for she united in an extraordinary degree mental power and emotional passion, checked and made more attractive by an inborn tact which had been cultivated till it amounted to genius, and she will remain a conspicuous and a pathetic figure among the extraordinary group of French women who are described comprehensively as the women of the salons.

MADAME GEOFFRIN

1699.   Birth of Marie Thérése Rodet, afterward Madame Geoffrin.

1713.   Marriage.

1715.   Birth of daughter, afterward the Marquise de la Ferté-Imbault.

1730.   Beginning of connection with the Marquise de Tencin.

1737.   Salon opened.

1749.   Death of Monsieur Geoffrin. Death of Madame de Tencin. Salon enlarged.

1777.   Death.

MADAME GEOFFRIN

I

MADAME GEOFFRIN is one of the most representative figures and forms one of the most interesting studies of the extraordinarily changing age, and its antagonistic elements, in which she lived. The old régime and the new ideas, rank and poverty, intellect and fashion, were mingled in her salon in seeming confusion and yet in a perfect harmony which cannot be realised unless we understand both her personality and the society over which she ruled.

Any study of the salon of Madame Geoffrin should be prefaced, however, by a sketch of another, that of Madame de Tencin, for the one would never have existed without the other. Not that the two women were alike; except that each possessed boundless ambition and unfailing persistency in the pursuit of her aims, no two persons could well be more dissimilar.

The Marquise de Tencin is as remarkable a personality as any one of the leaders of the salons from Madame de Rambouillet to Madame Necker, though it is the worst phase of her age, as well as its intelligence, which she exemplifies. In her is seen, in unparalleled measure, the clever, bold, unprincipled, designing woman of the world, who stops at nothing; for whom the time of the Regent and Louis XV was a golden age, and in which she was at once the most seductive and the most dangerous.[1]

One cannot but compare her with Madame Geoffrin who, on the contrary, made much of all the substantial virtues and whose life, which was contemporaneous with that of Louis XV, and passed, therefore, in the most dissolute and decrepit age of French history, and amidst surroundings the most unsettling to beliefs and morals,

[1] *Le Royaume de la rue Saint-Honoré*, par Pierre de Ségur, Paris, Calmann Lévy, 1898, p. 23.

Madame Geoffrin
From the painting attributed to Chardin in the Louvre
(By permission of Braun, Clément & Co.)

Madame Geoffrin

From the painting attributed to Chardin, in the Louvre

(By permission of Braun, Clement & Co.)

could, nevertheless, be cited, in any age, as a model of decorum. The Church, like the Court, presented a spectacle of laxity and venality which was without example, and the philosophers, who denounced the one and the other, were Madame Geoffrin's chosen companions, yet she remained stoutly loyal to existing conditions, always exacting respect for the prescribed law and order—in form, at least—even from these iconoclasts.

Madame de Tencin was born in 1681 and belongs, in period as in character, to the Regency. A nun who broke her vows, a canoness who forsook her charge, a mother who abandoned her child, a fine lady who was suspected to have connived at the murder of a troublesome lover, Madame de Tencin played a double part from the beginning to the end of her life, for she practised deceit to its greatest lengths. The poet Matthew Prior, when connected with the English embassy in Paris, was one of her first conquests; at another time she exerted all her uncommon fascinations of mind and body to bend the Duke of Orleans himself to her will, as she had done with many another, but the Regent, though licentious and extravagant, still had his own standard of conduct, and was not wanting in cleverness, and his favourites, however far they might lure him from the paths of rectitude, were never permitted to interfere in politics. On making this discovery, the Marquise, disappointed—her whole purpose in these undertakings being political,—turned her attention to Cardinal Dubois, from whom she hoped to gain more than had been vouchsafed by the Duke. She complaisantly descended therefore from master to minister, and with considerable success, for her brother, in whose interest she was working and for whom she gained the Cardinal's hat, Dubois soon discovered to be worth cultivating for his own sake.

In her youth Madame de Tencin was very pretty and she made the most of her physical charms in gaining control of men. But the waning of beauty with the passing of years necessitated a change of tactics, and she corrected her manner of living, relying upon her intellectual gifts alone to maintain her power. Her private life was henceforth one of the utmost propriety, being devoted to her salon, to her correspondence—in which Pope Benedict XIV figures,—and to writing clever, sentimental tales, where again the contradictory element in her character appears, for in these pages virtue and honour, aspiration, devotion and self-sacrifice are given the first place. In her salon she seemed at first, to the ordinary observer, the simple, accomplished housewife, always on the alert, first for the comfort and then for the interests of her guests. "She knew my tastes and always offered those dishes I preferred," sighed Fontenelle, when she died.

But simplicity and amiability were merely manner, pretensions to qualities which she did not possess but which served as a cloak to her astuteness and to the workings of a quick and powerful mind, for Madame de Tencin was keen and sound in her judgment, a woman in whom head took the place of heart.   Finesse and flattery, the success of which she openly and contemptuously boasted, were the arms to which she trusted.

She united, said Duclos, who was one of her intimates, all the different kinds of intellect, but she loved action and politics better than meditation and writing, and best enjoyed making use of the faculty which she possessed for directing affairs for the benefit of her friends, being particular neither in the object to be gained nor the means employed. Madame de Tencin gave her friends two dinners a week and two yards of velvet every New Year's day, besides sparing no pains to gain those more substantial favours which intrigue alone could bring about. She was the exploiter of Madame de Pompadour who, by her advice, was trained, from childhood, in such arts as would attract the King.   Madame de la Popelinière, the wife of the famous financier, also owed her rise in social status to Madame de Tencin's efforts ; Monsieur de la Popelinière had no idea of marrying the fascinating actress but Madame de

Tencin, to whom she appealed, through her influence at Court forced him to do so. Louis XV, however, warned by Fleury against the intriguing Cardinal and his sister, took a violent antipathy to Madame de Tencin; her very name, he said, made his flesh creep.

If Madame de Tencin had no other claim to fame she would still be a personage as the mother of d' Alembert. The story runs that she waited until he became famous before she would acknowledge their connection and that when, at last, she sent for the celebrated philosopher, and told him that he was her son, he replied that only the good woman who had brought him up had any claim to be his mother. It is unlikely, however, that Madame de Tencin ever troubled herself about d' Alembert living, as she left him nothing at her death.

Like her contemporaries Madame de Tencin must be judged by the standard of her time, when preferments were, as a rule, to be obtained only through intrigue, when abuses and scandals flourished openly in public and private life, when the fear of offending taste alone was recognised as any restraint on conduct and when, in the pursuit of pleasure, men and women attempted to drown their dissatisfaction in the present and their forebodings in regard to the future. But her contemporaries do not excuse Madame de Tencin. "She was born," writes Madame Du Deffand, "with the most fascinating qualities and the most abominable defects that God ever gave to one of his creatures." With the exception of Madame Geoffrin and of Mademoiselle Aïssé, who was under the protection of Madame de Tencin's sister, Madame de Ferriol, no women are ever mentioned in connection with her salon. Had Madame de Tencin, however, been altogether evil, she could never have gathered about her such men as the fastidious Fontenelle, who, after the death of the irreproachable Marquise de Lambert, found solace in her salon, or Mairan, the celebrated geometrician and physician, or Montesquieu, who here found inspiration for his great works. Bolingbroke and Lord Chesterfield were also among her assiduous frequenters.

Of such a character were her visitors. And the change in thought which led to the Revolution may be traced particularly to this salon where liberty of thought and speech—and this was wherein lay the secret of the power of the salons—was given full vent, for she encouraged discussion and loved learning in all its branches. I have said she was heartless, but she was passionately fond of her brother, the Cardinal de Tencin, who was as wicked as herself, and it was for him she risked her soul's salvation since, depraved as were the times, the Church still had a strong hold on most minds. Never rich, she yet never exerted herself to obtain money unless it were required for her brother's ambitious schemes. She was an excellent friend when to be so did not cross her own designs, losing no opportunity to help those she liked ; she piqued herself, indeed, on being a good friend and a bad enemy.

As time went on, poor in purse and weak in health, Madame de Tencin cast about for some one who could contribute to her failing resources and act as an auxiliary in her salon. A young woman who answered all her requirements was close at hand. Pretty, pious, intelligent, well-mannered, beneath her in station—which would make her easy to manage,—and with a prosperous old husband conveniently in the background, in Madame Geoffrin this astute woman found, in fact, without pay, the support which Madame Du Deffand at the same period of her life sought in Mademoiselle de Lespinasse.

And, until her death, nineteen years later, in 1749, their co-operation worked as well as one could wish though, perhaps, like the protégé of the other, this one also succeeded better than was liked; Madame Geoffrin equally attracted the choicest of the company to herself, the nucleus of the salon which was destined to become even more celebrated than that from which it sprung. Always good at prophecy, as her end drew near and Madame Geoffrin grew even more attentive, Madame de Tencin would cynically say to her intimates, "Do you know why she comes? It is to see what she can gather from my succession."

At Madame de Tencin's death Madame Geoffrin was fifty, but a few words must be given to her early life before studying the salon which is associated with her name.

II

Marie Thérèse Rodet, afterward Madame Geoffrin, was born in Paris, June 2, 1699. Her father had been a *valet de chambre* in the service of the Dauphiness. Her mother, the daughter of a banker, was a woman of superior talents. Both parents shortly died leaving her and an infant son to the care of the maternal grandmother, Madame Chemineau, who had decided and singular ideas on education and who undertook to put her quixotic theories into practice in the case of her granddaughter.

Madame Chemineau rightly believed that ability was certain to assert itself and that, without it, education was but a disagreeable make-believe which, in its ordinary acceptation, stifled originality. Only that which was natural could be agreeable or was right. It will thus be seen that Madame Chemineau was in advance of her time and that, in her philosophy, she forestalled Rousseau.

Thérèse, as she was called, had, therefore, no masters, but she was given books and taught to express her ideas concerning them. But this method, however far her intelligence may have been awakened by it, had its drawbacks, and she found herself a good deal handicapped, later in life, from want of knowledge of the simplest tools of speech, as well as of any kind of precise learning. Character, at all events, was assiduously cultivated, for Madame Chemineau spared no pains to inculcate in her granddaughter her own high-minded, if independent, manner of thinking. "My inner life," Madame Geoffrin wrote to Catherine of Russia, in 1765, "was as visible to her as my outward life; everything was a subject of instruction; my education was continual." Devout, in spite of some radical ideas, and a strict disciplinarian, Madame Chemineau was particular in all the practices of the Church, which she attended every day, and it was there that the young girl attracted the attention of her future husband.

The leaders of the salons, to judge by their portraits, were, more often than not, despite the picturesque, if unbecoming, dress of the time, decidedly plain, if not ugly, women. Madame Geoffrin, however, was an exception to the rule, though, by the time she arrived at celebrity, she had lost the fresh colour of youth and the serene, nun-like quality of the beauty which had distinguished her girlhood. It was an air of gentleness, aloofness, and simplicity as well as her large blue eyes and purity of complexion that won Monsieur Geoffrin's heart; had he been able to pierce the future and behold the imperious figure which the unfolding of the chrysalis brought forth, the marriage—which was celebrated July 14, 1713—would assuredly never have taken place.

The bride was fourteen, the bridegroom

forty-eight, but the disparity in years was
more than counterbalanced in the opinion
of the worldly-wise by the substantial character of the groom, who was a rich manu-
facturer and much considered in the parish.
The house—a legacy from a former marriage
—to which Monsieur Geoffrin took his young
wife was her home for the rest of her life.
It still stands on the rue Saint Honoré, nearly
opposite the chapel of the Assumption.

The interval between the marriage of
Madame Geoffrin and the beginning of
her relations with Madame de Tencin was
spent in the usual manifold and prosaic
details with which the *bourgeoise* of the
period busied herself; a diligent and careful housewife, an orderly and economi-
cal domestic system was rigidly enforced.
The daughter born two years after her
marriage became celebrated later as the
somewhat eccentric Madame de la Ferté-
Imbault. The care of her family and close
attention to church duties completely filled
the remainder of these physically active
and mentally tranquil days.

Such was her life and environment when, at thirty-one, Madame Geoffrin, without warning, turned, to her husband's dismay, completely aside from these homely and amiable occupations and entered into a con- nection which took her from home, and whose influence was soon felt in his quiet house, where persons quite unknown to Monsieur Geoffrin were entertained with unheard-of extravagance. It was plain that the happy obscurity in which he thought he was comfortably established for the rest of his days was seriously threatened. And Madame Geoffrin, whose thought, activity, and experience had hitherto been confined to domestic concerns and devotional exer- cises, received, except from his purse, no help from her husband in this new career which no sooner suggested itself than it was fully determined upon. On the contrary, Monsieur Geoffrin, now an elderly man, did not at all relish this interruption in his private life. Both by nature and principle, he heartily disliked and feared his wife's clever and free- thinking friends, and was therefore strongly opposed to this extraordinary departure. But the wife possessed the master mind, and the husband soon saw his remonstrances and himself equally put aside and that he must accommodate himself as best he might to his altered circumstances. Peace did not at once descend upon the house. For a few years Monsieur Geoffrin kept up a useless struggle and scenes of a violent character ensued whenever his wife demanded money. Finally, however, he succumbed to her stronger will and, in later years, a silent, unconsidered figure, a stranger to most of the company, who sat at Madame Geoffrin's well-filled table and conscientiously served her large parties, was the only visible evidence of Monsieur Geoffrin. One of her friends inquiring, after an absence, what had become of the old man who always sat at the foot of the table and who never said anything, she shortly replied : "It was my husband; he is dead." Madame de la Ferté-Imbault left one of those pen portraits, so much in vogue at the time, of Madame Geoffrin. Written long after her father's death, it thus refers to his subjugation : "She had a husband of ordinary understanding but rare by reason of his gothic virtues and by the goodness of his heart. She kept him always in fear in order to exercise her talent for conquest."

Madame Geoffrin was delivered in the same year from her politic, suspicious patroness and from the grumbling, parsimonious nonentity—so at least it would seem he appeared to her—who went by the name of her husband, and she succeeded without further question, as was foretold by the shrewd Marquise, to the salon of the one as well as to the possessions of the other.

As for the former she had surely earned some reward for she had served a long apprenticeship. A beautiful woman of thirty-one when Madame de Tencin befriended her, at her death she was fifty, had laid aside all pretensions to youth and beauty, and put on instead the cap which distinguished the elderly woman. Far from regretting the passing of youth with its agitations, she, on the other hand, welcomed the appearance of age with its promise of complete tranquillity. Like Madame de Lambert, Madame Geoffrin was afraid of the emotions, and she carefully suppressed any which may have been natural to her lest some unwonted pull at the heartstrings might trouble her repose.

To this excessive shrinking from any disturbance to her peace of mind is due the phenomenon of a woman anticipating more happiness for the sober decline of life than for the less temperate period of youth, and making haste to become old.

She did not agree, she wrote her friend Lady Hervey, in one of her characteristic letters filled with sound sense and worldly wisdom, with La Rochefoucauld, that old age was a tyrant to be dreaded. "Yes, for the foolish. But for the sensible I say that he is a wise governor who deprives us without effort, and before one is aware of it, of the taste for pleasures which are no longer suitable."[1]

The sober garb which Diderot so much

---

[1] Archives of the d' Estampes family. Cited by the Marquis de Ségur. Le Royaumé de la rue Saint Honoré, p. 98.

admired and which he describes in a letter to Mademoiselle Volland was therefore early assumed: "I always remark the noble and simple taste of her dress. It was, this day, a plain stuff of dark colour, with large sleeves, the linen the smoothest and finest, and then of the most exquisite freshness."

It must be said that society in France did not view old age or ill health in the same light in which it was regarded in England, and neither in the least prevented the utmost social activity and interest as long as life lasted. Horace Walpole, who crossed the Channel for the first time in the autumn of 1765, and who was confined to his room in Paris for the greater part of the winter by a bad attack of gout, where he was visited and alternately petted and scolded by Madame Geoffrin, wrote George Selwyn : "It is the country in the world to be sick and to grow old in. . . . Young people I conclude there are, but where they exist I don't guess ; not that I complain. It is charming to totter into vogue."[1] And so sensible Madame

[1] Letters of Horace Walpole. Dec. 2, 1765. Ed. Toynbee, vi., p. 367.

Geoffrin who, moreover, as I have already noted, practised the cult of the contented mind, was quite satisfied with the manner in which she had arranged her life.

And the sincerity of her statements was constantly proved. A flattering proposal of marriage at this time was met by the reply : "I am quite content with my society, with my situation, and with my name."

Madame Geoffrin had not long attained to a salon of her own at this time though, since 1737, an overflow which had constantly increased in numbers and importance, from Madame de Tencin's gatherings, had been accustomed to meet at her house on Wednesdays. After Monsieur Geoffrin's death, however, and that of Madame de Tencin, Madame Geoffrin came forward as a daring innovator and displayed the independence and originality of her mind by enlarging her coterie, which had hitherto been solely literary, through the introduction of painters, sculptors, and musicians, whom she received on Mondays and entertained at her artist dinners.

Purely artistic merit had never received such attention in a salon before and the novel and varied character which Madame Geoffrin by this means imparted to hers, attracted general attention. Distinguished strangers begged for introductions and princes, ambassadors, and the entire diplomatic circle flocked to her house asking to be received on the same simple footing as other guests. Therefore to the literary salon with its narrow confines, strict canons, and somewhat colourless lines, Madame Geoffrin added an artistic element which, together with the foreign group, gave to her salon a rich and cosmopolitan character.

The celebrity of the personage who has come down to us as the director of the salon which attracted the most attention in Europe, dates from this time, when Madame Geoffrin suddenly assumed that supreme position in society which she never lost, when a King called her by the familiar and endearing title of "Maman."

And so she was affectionately termed by many of her intimates. And it was as a parent, with troublesome but beloved children, that she scolded, and it is only in the character of children that her well grown but unruly family could take her sometimes meddlesome ministrations in good part.

When one considers the slow and careful preparation which Madame Geoffrin had received under her accomplished mentor, Madame de Tencin, and when to such instruction was united such ambition and such persistency in the pursuit of an object—for from the age of twenty she began consistently to plan her life—this triumphant début as Madame de Tencin's successor is not so surprising as it seems, but a mere matter of cause and effect. But the figure we see, though it is essentially French, is not a Frenchwoman such as we usually associate in our minds with the salons of Paris in the eighteenth century.

III

The remarkable friendship which united Madame Du Deffand and Horace Walpole was a connection between an old woman

and a man many years her junior. The
case is reversed with Madame Geoffrin and
Fontenelle, for he was forty-two years her
senior. Fontenelle was at the head of those
who took refuge with Madame Geoffrin
after the death of Madame de Tencin. With
Montesquieu and Voltaire, Fontenelle, before the death of Madame de Tencin had
deprived them of her salon, already knew
the agreeable interior where her habitués
had, for some time, been eagerly welcomed
by her intelligent protégé. The favourite
in three great salons, he was a faithful satel-
lite in the orbit of his new star as he had
been, first in that of Madame de Lambert,
and then of Madame de Tencin.

After Madame de Tencin, Fontenelle undoubtedly exercised the greatest influence
over Madame Geoffrin's mind and future,
though he was nearly seventy-five when
their courses met and she left her impression
his career. He had long been acknowledged
one of the most distinguished men of the age,
whose fame had continually increased with
years, and on whom time had left no trace.

19

Bernard de Bovier, better known as Fontenelle, was the nephew of Corneille, and was the link between him, Racine and Boileau, and Voltaire, Diderot and d' Alembert; between the old and the new thought, the old and the new periods of literature; for it was not alone in point of time that he connected them, he united also in himself the refinement, polish and distinction of the seventeenth and the scientific spirit of research and the philosophical bent of the eighteenth century.

If any man wishes to live to a green old age he should pattern after Fontenelle. Born in 1657, though he never looked strong he lived to be within a month of a hundred years, retaining throughout his long life perfect mental and, with the exception of the last few years, perfect physical health. He was free from vices, even from faults; he had, however, no passions to control, no troublesome warmth of temperament. Purely intellectual, no emotion ever disturbed him. He never laughed, never wept, was never angry. He was never even in a

FONTENELLE.

Né à Rouen le 11 Février 1657.
Mort à Paris le 5 Janvier 1757.

Engraved by St. Aubin from the Bust by le Moyne.

hurry. Naturally he never suffered. That a man likes his opposite was not true of Fontenelle who heartily disliked and even condemned any exhibition of emotion. "I have never experienced these violent agitations," he complained to Madame Geoffrin's fifteen-year-old daughter, put out by her gay spirits, "which makes me think they are unnatural."

This constitutional deficiency explains why his poetry should have offered itself to the satirist from Racine to Rousseau. Rousseau calls him "the daintiest pedant in the world." His subtle verse contains no feeling; his lovers, like himself, are calculating. But intellectually one of the most versatile of men, he early developed other capacities and was the first to bring scientific thought within popular reach by exchanging scientific phraseology for the vernacular. He was the first secretary of the Academy of Science—a post he filled from 1699 to 1741, having previously, at the age of thirty-four, been elected to the French Academy—to employ French in place of Latin, and all the while in his scientific and historical treatises, and even in his verse, is to be seen a philosophical tendency which constantly increases and by means of which, in the course of time, he outstripped in fame his critical literary contemporaries.

Poet, scientist, philosopher, universally admired and respected, Fontenelle has been likened to Voltaire in the scope of his talents but, with his peculiar temperament, it was inevitable that he should be wanting in spontaneity, frankness and freshness, those distinguishing qualities of Voltaire's genius, and beside him he is lifeless and dry. But as a writer of prose which, contrary to his semi-classical verse, is simple and unaffected, he was—though now little read—in his day eminently successful, and all his writings are characterised by his own individuality in their refinement, delicacy, and tact.

He was also remarkable as a conversationalist and then, at this time of his life, he had so much to say ! He had seen and talked with Madame de Sévigné and he had known the most distinguished men and women within the greater part of his century of existence. As a critic he was unexcelled, though, a lover of peace, he would never be drawn into a controversy. He especially had no mind to bring down the denunciation of the Church upon his head, and one of his productions arousing some discussion, he could not be got to defend his arguments, saying :

"I have no taste for polemics. Any quarrel displeases me. Let the devil be thought a prophet since the Jesuit father wishes it, and he believes it more orthodox."

For nearly twenty-five years Fontenelle spent several hours of each day with Madame Geoffrin but, in spite of their long and intimate association, they did not, surprising as it may seem, pretend to have a spark of affection for one another ; it was an intercourse merely agreeable and useful to each.

"Have you any regard for me?" she asked him one day. "I find you very amiable," he answered. "But if some one should tell you I had murdered one of my friends, would you believe it?" "I should wait," was the not too flattering reply.

Nevertheless these two remarkable persons concientiously fulfilled that which they considered to be their duty toward each other. No woman ever had a wiser counsellor or a more substantial friend and, for her part, she saw to his charities—for though he was not miserly he did not know how to give,—and she made him draw up a proper will, in which he named her his executrix; and when at last his time came to die, she sat by his bedside and took care, true to her ideas of propriety and prudence, that he—who never went to church—was duly confessed, and shriven, and made ready for Heaven. Up to the age of ninety-five he had been entirely free from infirmities, and even then he did not seem to feel them, and his accustomed serenity in no wise diminished. He died as he had lived, his last words, in answer to an inquiry if he were suffering, a tranquil dissent. "I do not suffer, but I feel a certain difficulty in existing."

Fontenelle is an extraordinary example of a life passed without expenditure of feeling. Above the ordinary frailties of men, unvexed by emotions, his mind alone was concerned, and at a time of life when most men begin to decline in vigour, when the day begins to lose its interest, and the individual, therefore, to become less interesting, this man was at the height of his power to please, of his fame and of his influence.

" He is all mind," said Madame Geoffrin, " He loves no one."

The philosopher found his friend intelligent and amiable. She admired his intellect and attached great value to his companionship. That was all; it was enough. Calm, cold, and calculating herself, Madame Geoffrin appreciated these features of her own character which were so strikingly developed in Fontenelle. He represented her ideal, and she consciously attempted to model herself after one to whom, in many

respects, she was akin. And she was remarkably successful. Though his influence
was not altogether for the best, for without
his elegance, her manners took on something of his indifference, unresponsiveness,
and a certain artificiality, all of which were
quite foreign to her, Sainte-Beuve pro-
nounces her to be a veritable Fontenelle in
her dislike of excess, of confusion, of passion in any form.[1] And in her prudence, in
the uniformity of her life, in her conception
of it, and in her strict adherence to her well-
considered plan of existence, she constantly
practised his precepts.

IV

Voltaire was one of Madame de Tencin's
friends who did not follow so readily the
general current which had set in toward
the salon of her successor. They were unsympathetic and quarrelled. His lawless
genius did not appeal to Madame Geoffrin's
practical mind. " The piece has some

[1] *Causeries du Lundi*, par Sainte-Beuve. Paris, Garnier Freres,
ii., p. 319

beauty," she said of *Rome Vaincue*, "but
not common-sense, like everything he does."
And he, on his side, ridiculed the pretensions
of a woman who could not write "two
lines correctly" to pose as the patroness of
letters. Yet he appreciated her capacity
and her quality of trustworthiness and
when, after the death of Fontenelle, a disappointed relative violently attacked her
reputation and attempted to break the will,
Voltaire came to her defence and thenceforward they always remained on friendly,
if not cordial, terms.

The relations of Madame Geoffrin with
Montesquieu took a contrary course. Much
of her success was due to him, but his faith
in her received a shock at the discovery
that she pretended to a knowledge of his
work which she did not possess. The coldness which then ensued was followed later
by a complete rupture when he took the
part of his protégé, l'abbé de Guasco, when
she refused to receive him, a proceeding
which, though she was quite justified, had
disagreeable consequences, for twelve years

after Montesquieu's death, the abbé, who had nourished his resentment, published, under the title *Lettres familières du Président de Montesquieu,* a work purporting to be authentic letters from the celebrated writer to Guasco, in which Madame Geoffrin and her pretensions were ridiculed in a most offensive way. Her reputation and influence were such, however, that, with the aid of the Duc de Choiseul, then in power, she succeeded not only in having the copies which had been issued destroyed, but the book was officially branded as false. Not even then content, she went so far as to have a new edition printed in which, of course, the defamatory letters were omitted. Such had been the simplicity and discretion of Madame Geoffrin's life and manners that she had disarmed envy and had few enemies and this is the only instance of really malevolent attack from which she had to suffer throughout her long career.

Madame Geoffrin was an exacting friend with fixed ideas of values. To live with her on terms of peace one must learn to bend

MONTESQUIEU.
After the Painting by Deveria.

absolutely to her will. Piron, the epigram-
matist, was another of her early supporters
with whom she quarrelled. In this case it was
habitual for they no sooner were reconciled
than they quarrelled again and their friendship, though it lasted nearly forty years, was
never anything more than half-hearted on
either side. "I have just left," Piron wrote
a friend, "a hôtel de Rambouillet, where the
lady of the house gives dinners to all the illustrious parasites of our three Academies.
. . . No one knows anything but she
and her friends, among whom I have not, I
believe, the honour to be. I only figure in
this fine landscape as a kind of barbarian."
In truth, the bold unknown who, on his
arrival in Paris, concealed behind the scenes
of the little market theatres, put such
pointed and biting epigrams into the mouths
of the marionettes that the police were ordered to interfere ; whose wit and wisdom
were crystallised in bon mots and epigrams
whenever he spoke ; the author of the line
"J' ai ri, me voila désarmé," so significant,
after all, of a good-natured philosophy ; the

"talking machine" as Grimm called the antagonist before whose scathing satire even Voltaire winced and of whose words every one, with the exception of Madame Geoffrin, stood in fear ; such a man could ill brook the scolding and complaints, the criticisms, cuttings, and clippings—the various processes by which Madame Geoffrin attempted to fashion her friends to her liking.

After Fontenelle, the oldest and most cherished friend of Madame Geoffrin was Mairan, who was a member of every learned society in Europe. He was a counterpart in many ways of Fontenelle, whom he succeeded as perpetual secretary to the Academy of Sciences. Both living to a great age had descended from the salon of Madame de Lambert in the previous century to that of Madame de Tencin, and then to Madame Geoffrin. He belonged to the psychological type which appealed so strongly to Madame Geoffrin, for he was as far above the turmoil of the passions as herself or Fontenelle. Neither, like Fontenelle, did he undertake to disturb

the tranquillity of his existence by contract-
ing domestic ties, and when he died, at the
age of ninety-three, full of respect and honours as of years, she watched by his bedside
as she had by that of Fontenelle, and was as
zealous for his soul's welfare and that he
should make as decorous an end. And she
was as successful, for he also at her desire
now confessed and took communion for the
first time. He also testified his devotion by
his will, in which he left her all his considerable fortune. Again, as in the former case, she
relinquished all personal benefit from this
bequest and divided everything between his
relatives, old domestics, and needy writers.

Another who occupied an important place
in Madame Geoffrin's life, and also a member
of this literary group, was Burigny, the historian, her "major domo." Forever at her beck
and call, by turns scolded and petted, his
life must at times have been a burden. "It
is forty years since I have been your servant," he exclaimed one day, his patience
exhausted, "and at least thirty-nine since I
have been your slave!" She perhaps scolded

him more than any one, which leads one to believe that she probably preferred him. Following the example of Fontenelle and Mairan, Burigny, too, never married, and as he and Madame Geoffrin advanced in years, she insisted that he should make her house his home. It would seem as though these scholars had in their researches discovered the secret of longevity; Burigny lived to be nearly a hundred—surviving Madame Geoffrin—without ills or infirmities of any kind. Among the many friends with whom Madame Geoffrin and her daughter were surrounded, Burigny and Grimm alone were able to live on cordial terms with each, and after Madame Geoffrin's death the former still lived on with Madame de la Ferté-Imbault. The manner of death of this happy, peaceable, equable old man, who did not feel or fear its approach any more than that of sleep, shows that the philosophical circle were not all wanting in religious feeling. When, his strength ebbing, he was urged to take food, he answered, smiling :

"I am not anxious for it, for I am, I confess, curious to see more nearly the eternal Father."

V

Madame de Rambouillet permanently raised the status of men of letters and to Madame Geoffrin belongs the credit of performing the same service for painters, sculptors, and musicians. Once more society opened its ranks in order that its intellectual scope might be still further increased. Ambitious to extend her dominions, Madame Geoffrin, who had become a ruler of society, enlarged the boundaries of her salon by reinforcing the literary group—which had been gradually coming to the front, superseding even the men of rank who had pretensions to birth alone—with those whose professions hitherto had been held unworthy to be ranked with literature.

It cannot be said, however, generous as were her instincts, that it was pure benevolence, either for artists or for society in general, which inspired Madame Geoffrin's efforts ; primarily, she was blind to these

larger aims, and was working for her own
aggrandisement. Devoured by a colos-
sal ambition, she made use of all her practical intelligence to further her ends. A
simple bourgeoise by birth, and without
education, she aspired to, and succeeded in
becoming, the queen of an intellectual realm
whose confines should not be bounded by
Paris, or even France, but which should extend throughout Europe.

Madame Geoffrin sought to supply the
defects—all too patent—of her early education by elementary tasks, taking, for instance, lessons to improve her handwriting.
She seems, however, to have read few of
the works of the intellectual giants of the
time and her frank remark to the learned
Burigny, when he gave her his works,
"I am glad to have them, but I do not
want to read them," probably might have
been said to most of the men of letters
from whom she received such gifts. Pictures pleased her more than books and she
paid more attention to them, following
closely the work of the painters whom she

patronised, picking flaws without stint, worrying and wearying them with her insistent advice which, nevertheless, though always after violent discussions, she made them follow. Sometimes her protégés absolutely refused to submit to her arbitrary counsels, as when Boucher sent a picture which he had undertaken, under her surveillance, for the King of Poland, to Wien to be finished. And Greuze threatened to immortalise her, after one of these tumultuous scenes, as a tyrannical schoolmistress, whip in hand. But, strange as it may seem, as a rule, all these remarkable men submitted, sooner or later, and with more or less good grace, to this despotic sway, and their conflicts became less frequent and reconciliations more certain as she learned to understand the artist's temperament, and so criticised less and praised more. "I have become their friend because I see them often, make them work, caress them, praise them, and pay them very well," she wrote to the King of Poland, in 1766, and in these last words may be found, it is

possible, the ultimate reason for their submission.

But the success of the Monday dinners
was not due to her alone, she was assisted
in their formation by the Count de Caylus,
one of the most original and contradictory
characters who shines in this salon ; a man
who went to curious extremes, who re-
nounced the aristocracy into which he was
born, who heartily disliked the philosophers
and encyclopédistes, and who despised, for
the most part, men of letters.   An antiqua-
rian, an art connoisseur, himself an engraver,
he cared only, as a rule, for the society
of artists.   It was he who selected the
new recruits, and who persuaded Madame
Geoffrin that they should have a day of their
own when they—and he—would be entirely
independent of her literary friends.

In spite of his emphatic protests, however,
she soon undertook to leaven this too one-
ideaed society by the introduction of a few
amateurs such as the Marquis de Marigny,
Madame de Pompadour's brother ; the Duc
de la Rochefoucauld, Marmontel, d'Alem-

bert, and others from her Wednesday literary
coterie were admitted, and the reputation
of the Mondays soon rivalled that of
the Wednesdays. The Mondays, nevertheless, always retained the distinctive artistic
character which belongs to no other salon.

A letter from a youthful *débutant* in the
world of art, Costa de Beauregard, gives an
idea of how they occupied themselves :

There were at dinner [he wrote], M. de Marigny, the Duc de la Rochefoucauld, Marmontel,
Cochin, the celebrated engraver, and many other persons, whose names I don't know. Each one had
brought something: Vernet a picture that had just
come from Italy, and which they thought was by Cor-
reggio; M. de la Rochefoucauld, a little picture
painted "en camieu" and encrusted by a process
of which no one knew; M. Mariette, a little port-
folio filled with his most beautiful prints; M. Cochin,
some pen and ink sketches; and I, my picture. . . .
Madame Geoffrin has a brusque and lively manner. For
the daughter of a *valet de chambre* of the Dauphiness
she appears to me very much at her ease in the midst
of these grand seigneurs and great minds.[1]

She read letters, he continues, from the
King of Poland and Voltaire, and toward the
end of the dinner a decrepit old gentleman,

[1] *Le Royaume de la rue Saint Honoré*, p. 62.

on the arm of a domestic, was announced.
It was Président Hénault, Madame Du Deffand's old friend, now aged eighty-two and
still, according to our chronicler, in spite of
years and deafness, " charmingly gay."

Nor was music wanting to add to the
charm of these reunions ; musicians were
made as welcome as artists, and one of the
portraits of Madame Geoffrin represents her
listening to a performer, supposed to be
Rameau, playing on the clavecin. Naturally,
therefore, when the child Mozart appeared
in Paris Madame Geoffrin was one of the
first to appreciate his precocious genius; he
played before her, and when he left Paris
for Vienna she forestalled his arrival by
letters of recommendation to the Austrian
Minister.

Among her artists were Boucher, gay, gallant, and talkative; La Tour, the pastellist,
a striking contrast, with his melancholy
humour and philanthropic occupations, to
the pleasure-loving Boucher, one the true
artistic Bohemian type, the other many-
sided, and an artist on one side only; Bou-

chardon, the sculptor, and Langrenée and Drouais, then so popular, might also have been seen in her salon.

But it was Carle Van Loo, Boucher's gifted pupil, of whom Madame Geoffrin was especially fond.   Regularly every week she paid a visit to the studio of her painter " attitré," as he was called.   These visits, invariably accompanied by differences of opinion, by laughter and tears, were of a particularly tempestuous description.

Two of Van Loo's most celebrated works, *La Conversation Espagnole* and *La Lecture*, in both of which the portrait of Madame Geoffrin's daughter appears, were painted under these trying conditions.

Madame Geoffrin's large collection of pictures, comprising no less than sixty-three works of the best artists of the period and all executed under her supervision, show that this practical woman knew how to give effective shape to her interest in art and in her friends.

The celebrated *carnets* which she kept, wherein were minutely described the main transactions of her life, form not alone a social encyclopædia of the time but a catalogue of her expenditures. In one place we read of "Mr. Wilkes, English, ugly, false, and very extraordinary, who has been much talked about in London." And in another that she gave Van Loo eighteen thousand livres for three pictures for her bedroom.

It will be seen that Madame Geoffrin was a kind of benevolent despot in her dealings with artists, her habitual generosity removing the sting from her criticisms. She always paid for her pictures above their market value, and the same generosity was shown not only by her purchases but by her interest in the artists' families, and if death deprived them of the bread winner, Madame Geoffrin invariably came to their assistance.

I must touch on another incident in the life of Madame Geoffrin in which—and it is difficult to find a quarter in mid or late eighteenth century society, on either side the channel, where his name is not found—

Horace Walpole appears, and not to his advantage.

Introduced by Lady Hervey, the admirer and correspondent of each, he was received at once on the footing of a friend, and until he met Madame Du Deffand he could not say enough in her praise. " I have been with Madame Geoffrin several times," he wrote Lady Hervey soon after his arrival, and "I think she has one of the best understandings I ever met, and more knowledge of the world."[1] The good opinion he had conceived of her even increased, and Madame Geoffrin succeeded in evoking something which appeared like real enthusiasm, for in a short time he again wrote : "I make her both my confessor and director, and begin to think I shall be a reasonable creature at last, which I had never intended to be. . . . If it was worth her while, I assure your Ladyship she might govern me like a child."[2]

[1] Oct. 3, 1765, *Letters of Horace Walpole*, ed., Toynbee, vi., p. 306.

[2] Oct. 13, 1765, *Letters of Horace Walpole*, ed., Toynbee, vi., p. 322.

But with the advent of Madame Du Deffand Walpole's ardour for Madame Geoffrin rapidly cooled.   And what chance for success did the bourgeoise, in whom were apparent many characteristics of her vulgar origin, have, in the imagination of an æsthetic connoisseur like Walpole, against the charm of a woman an aristocrat *in esse* as was Walpole himself?

Madame Du Deffand's profound and subtle intellect and her good breeding, all of which was reflected in her salon, satisfied both Walpole's taste and understanding, and the fond and singular attachment of an old woman and a celebrity appealed strongly to the many odd instincts which were cultivated so assiduously in the Strawberry Hill dilettante—and Walpole was not apt to deny himself anything he liked.

The generous impulses which agitated the philosophical group in the salon of Madame Geoffrin were incomprehensible to Walpole's somewhat narrow and timid order of mind; it was to be expected, therefore, that when he had to choose between the two women he should renounce Madame Geoffrin. It was not, however, a change of heart of which Madame Geoffrin had reason to complain, for the prince of gossips, never able to hold his tongue, now began to criticise her most unkindly. In January, 1766, he sent the following lifelike sketch to the poet Gray which cannot be said to be obscured by any halo of friendship:

Madame Geoffrin, of whom you have heard much, is an extraordinary woman, with more common sense than I almost ever met with. Great quickness in discovering characters, penetration in going to the bottom of them, and a pencil that never fails in a likeness —seldom a favourable one. She exacts and preserves, spite of her birth and their nonsensical prejudices about nobility, great court and attention. This she acquires by a thousand little arts and offices of friendship ; and by a freedom and severity, which seem to be her sole end of drawing a concourse to her ; for she insists on scolding those she inveigles to her. She has little taste and less knowledge, but protects artisans and authors, and courts a few people to have the credit of serving her dependents. She was bred under the famous Madame Tencin, who advised her never to refuse any man; for, said her mistress, though nine in ten should not care a farthing for you, the tenth may live to be an useful friend. She did not adopt or reject the whole plan, but fully retained the purport of the maxim. In short she is an epitome of empire, subsisting by rewards and punishments.[1]

Walpole later went so far as to advise his friends to avoid her. "Indeed, you would be sick of that house," he wrote General Conway, "whither all the pretended *beaux esprits* and *faux savants* go, and where they are very impertinent and dogmatic."[2]

It is not probable, however, that Madame Geoffrin, surrounded by men of the first intellectual rank, long mourned Walpole the dilettante. At this very time, also, her mind was occupied with her projected visit to Stanislaus II, King of Poland, whom, when a youth of twenty-one, she had rescued from a debtor's prison.

In those days he possessed no pretensions to the throne. His father, Count Poniatowski, indicated the esteem in which Madame Geoffrin was held by sending five sons in succession to the rue Saint Honoré, with instructions to obey her as if she were their

[1] *Letters of Horace Walpole*, ed., Toynbee, vi., p. 404.

[2] Sept. 28, 1774. *Letters of Horace Walpole*, ed., Toynbee, ix. p. 59.

mother, and when, in 1753, the fourth son attained his majority and came, in his turn, to visit Paris, he proceeded, like his brothers, straightway to this hospitable house, and their relations from that time were those of mother and son. Of course, she scolded him for his extravagance and of course she paid his debts. He was affectionate and hearkened to her advice. Four years later he was elected to the throne of Poland through the good offices of Catherine II, who had been violently in love with him, but, perfectly recovered, had thrown him a kingdom to assuage his sorrow.

In everything which relates to Poniatowski Madame Geoffrin is seen in a new rôle, and the whole-hearted way in which she surrendered herself to this attachment is an idiosyncrasy in her self-contained and egotistical nature.

Hardly able to contain her joy at the unexpected turn of Fortune's wheel, she lost her customary balance, and appears even in a somewhat ridiculous aspect. "My dear son, my dear King, my dear Stanislaus-

Auguste, my trinity," were the extravagant terms in which she addressed the young monarch.

Her desire to see her protegé must indeed have been strong, for a journey to Warsaw before the time of railways, when there were scarcely roads of any description on many parts of the route, was no light undertaking for any ordinary woman nearly seventy years of age. But at sixty-seven Madame Geoffrin's intellectual faculties were at their best, and she was as vigorous in body as in mind when, on May 1, 1766, to the indignation of her society, who felt themselves much injured, she left Paris for the Polish capital.

The journey was a series of triumphs. Everywhere her approach, heralded in advance, was the signal for attentions without number. On the eve of her departure from Vienna she wrote her daughter in the following enthusiastic strain:

The Court and the town have overwhelmed me with kindness. I have seen the Emperor, the Empress-Queen, the Archdukes, and the Archduchesses, with the same ease that I do the persons who do me the

honour to come to see me. All the Imperial family,
each one separately, has said to me the most flattering things in the world. The Prince de Kaunitz,
first minister . . . has overwhelmed me with
attentions. I have hardly left his house, which is the
. . . most brilliant that one can imagine. [And
she concludes naively:] You see beautiful Marquise,
that you have a mother who is worthy of this
honour.[1]

The traveller was invited to Schönbrunn
where she saw, for the first time, Marie An-
toinette, then a girl of twelve and whom
Madame Geoffrin thought "beautiful as an
angel." Something of the fate of the future
Queen of France was foreshadowed in the
conversation which followed. "What a
charming little Archduchess!" exclaimed
the visitor, who—as she wrote—felt quite at
home, "How I would like to carry her off
with me!" "Take her, take her!" was
the reply, and Maria Theresa afterwards even
suggested to Madame Geoffrin that she
should make known her happy impressions
in France. It must not be thought, however, from this incident, that Madame Geof-

[1] *Le Royaume de la rue Saint-Honoré*, pp. 259, 260.

frin had any influence at the French Court, whose etiquette, the most strict in Europe, effectually checked the indulgence of any political aspirations in a woman of the bourgeoisie, no matter how influential—unless, indeed, she chanced to catch the fancy of the King.

If they have talked of my travels in Paris, I assure you they have talked still more about them in Vienna. All the ladies said there was nothing they would not give to see my meeting with the King. They would have been satisfied. When I saw the King at the foot of his steps, crying *Voila Maman!* and seizing me in his arms, the beating of my heart and the trembling of my knees so affected me that I should have fallen if the King had not supported me.[1]

So, on her arrival in Warsaw, again wrote Madame Geoffrin to her daughter, still in the first flush of happiness and satisfied pride. But her tone soon changed. In spite of her pleasure in the society of her beloved "son," and in the reflected glory which she enjoyed in Poniatowski's court, Madame Geoffrin's visit to Warsaw proved to be a disappointment. Many fond illusions were dispelled and a conversion was ex-

[1] *Le Royaume de la rue Saint Honoré*, p. 265.

perienced in respect to royalty from which she never recanted.

Bad as was the state of affairs in France, there were countries where a worse condition prevailed. "All that I have seen since leaving home makes me thank God that I was born French and a private person," she wrote d'Alembert. The friend of philosophers and a woman sprung from the bourgeoisie could not behold, untouched, the misery of the poor, the debasement of the middle class, and the arrogance of the nobles, which existed in Poland. Accustomed to advise and scold, she still scolded, and suggested impossible reforms to the King, who, first the toy and then the tool of Catherine, possessed no initiative and very little authority. Like some feeble, profligate, oriental potentate he was permitted every luxury, or excess, as he liked, but Catherine did not wish reforms for Poland and Madame Geoffrin found her hero, whom she had apotheosised as a Sully and a Henri IV, at the head of the worst governed kingdom in Europe. Well meaning, polished, charming, Poniatowski was but a mere puppet in the hands of a strong, unprincipled, and ambitious autocrat. His reign was the antithesis of Madame Geoffrin's expectations and she made no attempt to conceal her dissatisfaction. The forbearance of the King alone prevented a quarrel. But a peace was patched up, the King even persuading her to prolong her stay for a little, as the time set for her departure approached. The final parting was tender on his part and affectionate on hers, though she refused the princely gifts which he pressed upon her, accepting only his miniature from which she detached the diamonds in which it was framed.

Madame Geoffrin's visits to Vienna and Warsaw had fired the imagination of the friends she had left behind much as Poniatowski's elevation to the throne had her own; and with similar results. Voltaire, full of philanthropical zeal wrote, before she left, begging her to use her influence with the King that he might also come to the succour of the persecuted. Marmontel, in extravagant terms, foretold the most improbable consequences for the benefit of humanity from her travels.

But if, in these ways, her journey disappointed her friends and herself, this year marked the culminating point of her triumphs and on her return, in October, the wanderer was received like a sovereign returning to his own.

Her name had attained a European reputation and she was recognised everywhere as a power in society. It was even said that the German courts sent spies to report on the drift of opinion in her salon. Such a centre of influence had the hôtel in the rue Saint Honoré become.

Her personal relations with the continental courts is a striking proof of the wide extent of the conquests of the ambitious bourgeoise. Gustavus III continued in Stockholm, by means of letters, an intimate intercourse begun in Paris before his accession. Her correspondence with Catherine II, begun by the Empress for political reasons, soon, despite the unwelcome obsequiousness of Madame Geoffrin's first letters, struck a sympathetic chord.

Do not say, I beg of you [she wrote, in 1765], that your letters are long, with your fine tact you should have felt long ago that I devour these letters; and that, from beginning to end I have equal pleasure in reading and re-reading them. They are charming, if I were a man, I should say ravishing, and that is true.[1]

Another time the sovereign repeats a request that Madame Geoffrin should abandon the humble attitude so foreign to her nature. "Arise, Madame, here is my hand. It is so that I propose to reply in future to your prosternations, genuflexions, etc., to stop them." But the unbecoming mask of humility which Madame Geoffrin—always dazzled by the glitter of a great title—assumed for exalted persons, was soon cast aside, and her true character disclosed ; and the Czarina was forced to submit to the same censorious criticisms that were meted out to all those whom Madame Geoffrin pretended to love.

Though Madame Geoffrin's letters have,

---

[1] *Le Royaume de la rue Saint-Honoré*, pp. 442, 443.

with the exception of a few fragments, dis-
appeared, those of the Empress remain to
reveal the evolution of one of the strangest
friendships which ever existed between two
celebrated women. Widely separated in
station, they were united and were alike in
their masculine minds, their imperious and
uncontrolled wills, and their absolutely independent positions, for Madame Geoffrin
was as autocratic and all-powerful in her
sphere of influence as was the ruler of all
the Russias within her dominions.

Their correspondence lasted, with some
breaks, for five years, though their relations
were considerably strained by Madame
Geoffrin's visit to Warsaw, of which she
left Catherine, who had frequently and in-
sistently urged her to visit St. Petersburgh,
in ignorance ; and when, after the traveller's
return, the Empress learned that a political
paper by Rulhière, secretary to the French
minister at St. Petersburgh, which she had
in vain tried to suppress, and wherein the
doubtful means she had employed to gain
possession of her throne were freely dis-

cussed, had been read in Madame Geoffrin's salon, all communication between the
celebrated bourgeoise and the notorious
Empress came to an end.

Some attempt has been made[1] to defend
this questionable proceeding on the part of
a friend by attributing to Madame Geoffrin
the belief that the work which drew, after
all, a flattering portrait of the Empress,
would add to, rather than detract from, her
reputation. The paper, however, which
was never publicly circulated, had been
read in Madame Du Deffand's salon, which
was enough, probably, to fire Madame Geoffrin with jealous zeal that her society also
should taste the dangerous fruit which
Madame Du Deffand's guests had enjoyed.

IX

What are the prominent names, beside
those which have been mentioned, to be
found in Madame Geoffrin's salon ? Among
her first followers were Marivaux, Fonte-

[1] De Ségur, *Le Royaume de la rue Saint Honoré*, pp. 221–22.

nelle's disciple, and the poet Saurin. Then came " pére " Paciaudi, the well-known correspondent of the Comte de Caylus, and his companion in archæological research ; the abbés Raynal, Galiani, and Morellet, the first of whom opened the correspondence with the German courts which Grimm afterward developed, the second, the gay little Neapolitan, Madame d' Épinay's correspondent who, from the time he was introduced was never absent from a single one of Madame Geoffrin's Wednesdays as long as he was in Paris. Wig awry, hands and feet or piercing voice never still, Galiani was one of the features of Madame Geoffrin's salon. "I love her, I respect her, I adore her ; and if they listened to me I would always talk of her !" he wrote Madame Necker of their mutual friend, for Madame Geoffrin, though she never, with one exception, invited a woman to her dinners, was not without women friends. Galiani, forever exiled, constantly lamented the loss of the brilliant salons of Paris. "There is no way of making Naples resemble Paris if we do not find a woman to guide us, to *Geoffrinise* us," he cried.

Marmontel, whom she launched on the career of letters, and Morellet, Helvétius, and d'Holbach gave dinners which were something in the nature of rivals to her own, in her later years; the strong feelings which the times engendered and which were forbidden utterance by Madame Geoffrin were there given free play, and religion and politics were discussed with all the vehemence which these subjects naturally aroused. Hume, the friend and correspondent of Julie de Lespinasse, was also a friend and correspondent of Madame Geoffrin, and her letters to him contain a personal note which is not often found in her writing. Madame Necker brought Gibbon. The Comte de Creutz, the Swedish Minister, a lover of the fine arts, was also of the number, and Gatti, the celebrated Italian doctor; Diderot, as well, whom, though Madame Geoffrin assisted, she never appreciated; Saint Lambert, Madame d'Houdetot's lover; Turgot, Thomas, and Suard, the journalist, whose marriage, against Madame Geoffrin's advice, to a girl as gifted but as penniless as himself, so irritated her that two years passed before she would speak to them.

Late in her life but, with the exception of Poniatowski, first in her heart, came d'Alembert and Julie de Lespinasse, waifs and strays from Madame Du Deffand's salon. D'Alembert, though drawn from his obscurity and introduced to society by Madame Geoffrin, had long been a wanderer from her ranks and had for many years taken the leading part in Madame Du Deffand's salon and occupied the first place in her affections. Now, refusing to forsake Julie and, therefore, cast forth with her, he sought help from his old friend.

Julie de Lespinasse was the only woman ever admitted to Madame Geoffrin's dinners; women, Madame Geoffrin said, invariably diverting attention from conversation to themselves.

But this conviction did not prevent her from cultivating women. She began a new fashion by inviting company for the middle of the day, but for her women friends, whom she chose from the highest aristocracy, she had supper parties. She was particularly intimate with Madame de la Vallière until senility overtook the Duchess, the robust bourgeoise being still in the enjoyment of all her faculties. Catherine of Russia and Lady Hervey proved that Madame Geoffrin could make friends among women abroad and, especially during the last years of her life, she made many at home.

Madame Necker, young, beautiful, and clever, attracted many of the habitués of Madame Geoffrin's salon to her own, but no trace of jealousy is ever to be found in Madame Geoffrin and she cordially welcomed the new candidate to the philosophical circle. They visited each other without ceremony, and Monsieur and Madame Necker were both counted among her favourites.

When, in 1764, turned out of doors by Madame Du Deffand, Julie de Lespinasse was led by d'Alembert to Madame Geoffrin, the interesting fugitive from the rival salon was warmly welcomed and unexampled attentions and benefits were heaped upon her. The warmth of Madame Geoffrin's welcome was prompted at first, there is no doubt, by spite towards the common enemy, but she soon experienced the ascendency of that charm which all those underwent who ever came in contact with Julie de Lespinasse and fell likewise a willing victim to her spells.

As I have said, Poniatowski apart, Julie de Lespinasse and d'Alembert were those to whom Madame Geoffrin became most deeply attached, and it was they to whom she turned as she grew older and feebler. The daily visits which at first they paid her together were increased to two a day and, finally, even the task of selecting her guests was abandoned to them, notwithstanding the growing jealousy of Madame Geoffrin's opposing and imposing daughter who could only see in Julie de Lespinasse and d'Alembert a dangerous, conspiring pair and in their devotion a carefully woven intrigue directed against herself, and which had pecuniary gain for its object.

Madame Geoffrin, as we know, survived Julie de Lespinasse, who, unknown to Madame Geoffrin, as to her other friends, was consumed by the unsatisfied longings of a passionate heart and, the year following her death, Madame Geoffrin falling ill, the combative daughter had her own way and gained the satisfaction of denying admittance to d'Alembert.

Illness had not destroyed Madame Geoffrin's strong sense of humour. "She wished to defend my tomb against the infidels!" she said later, laughing, for d'Alembert was not the only philosopher against whom Madame de la Ferté-Imbault shut their door, being equally severe in regard to all Madame Geoffrin's philosophical friends and, to avoid a conflict with the high-spirited Marquise, Madame Geoffrin was obliged to acquiesce in this hard measure. Great was the scandal it occasioned; her old friends, resenting this treatment provoking a violent quarrel with the Church party who, on their side, warmly defended the action of the zealous Marquise.

In Madame Geoffrin's carefully premeditated scheme of existence she had by no means forgotten to plan for her old age. "At seventy," she said, "I shall begin to break all the attachments of my heart, then I will firmly seal it in a manner that none shall enter."

This determination could be the only reason for her behaviour toward Poniatowski when, in 1768, she returned all his letters and endeavoured to provoke a rupture. But the King again refused to quarrel and after a time their correspondence was resumed. She henceforth declined to receive any new-comers and her salon began to shrink as she endeavoured to detach herself from the various interests of life.

"You have said, my dear Grimm, that the baron was very amiable," she wrote touchingly, in 1770, excusing herself from receiving him, "It is another reason to fortify myself in my resolution to make no more acquaintances. The gate is closed."

Madame Geoffrin was by nature optimistic and she had always possessed what she called an "inward gaiety." She had not been one of those who regarded the growing public discontent with anxiety, but now her tone begins to change and her thoughts are tinged with melancholy. "At this moment they are destroying ; we must see what they will reconstruct on the ruins. Young, one trusts ; old, one waits," she wrote on her "carnets."

Neither did Madame Geoffrin neglect precautionary measures for the salvation of her soul in her methodical preparations. "She went to church," said Marmontel, satirically, referring to her clandestine attendance at mass, "to gain with Heaven without losing with her world." But Madame Geoffrin had always forbidden open attacks against the Church and even sometimes sought to bring her philosophical friends into harmony with it, as in the case of Fontenelle and of Mairan ; and she now wished no less to make the same good end herself. At all events, from this time she attended church oftener and it was this new devotional zeal which hastened her death.

The Papal Jubilee of 1776 was celebrated with extraordinary fervour in Paris. There was a religious revival and even many who agreed with the encyclopédistes were carried away by the wave of feeling which swept over the city. Though it was March, the cold was unprecedented, and Madame Geoffrin was among the pious who remained for many hours at church exposed to the trying cold, from the effects of which she never recovered.

The idea of old age is usually associated in the mind with dependence and trust, the drawing closer of the bonds which unite families, but family ties were early relegated to the background by Madame Geoffrin, and anything which resembles affection must be looked for in the case of Poniatowski, whom she called her son, rather than of her daughter, maternal instinct had not been strong enough to override an antagonism

arising from opposing ideals and clashing of
wills. The relations between mother and
daughter were maintained by reason rather
than by affection, and were in the nature
of the armed peace which constitutes the
so-called friendly relations between jealous
neighbouring nations, but, as they grew
older, each felt the estrangement, and better
feelings were cultivated between them.

Madame de la Ferté-Imbault, though she
early lost her husband, was lifted, by reason
of her marriage, to the ranks of the noblesse,
and she identified herself completely with
the Court. Like her mother, she possessed
uncommon virtues for her time and was ex-
emplary in her private life. The two, however, never agreed, and she undoubtedly
added more of pain than pleasure to the
sum of Madame Geoffrin's life, and was of
no more assistance to her in her career
than her husband had been. The daughter, in fact, detested the philosophers as
heartily as had her father, and openly declared her aversion to the profession of
letters. Madame de la Ferté-Imbault not

only practised exceptional virtues in a time of
lax behaviour but in a time, also, of unbelief
she was an uncompromising member of the
church militant, and denounced the encyclopédistes with characteristic energy as "se-
ductors, corruptors, and destroyers of all
virtue and of all principle."

Madame de la Ferté-Imbault was no less
worthy of her mother in mind than in
morals, as was proved by the character of
her friendships which included men such as
Maurepas, Cardinal de Bernis, and the Duc
de Nivernais, who were the leaders of the
anti-philosophical party; but they were intimacies which did not tend to union between two self-willed natures living under
the same roof.

D'Alembert declared that Madame de la
Ferté-Imbault curried favour with the aristocracy and it is true that, after the example of
her mother, she sought intimacies with the
great. One of these was her friendship with
the old and exiled though still gay and gallant
King Stanislas Leczinski — Poniatowski's
predecessor and the father of Louis XV.'s

Queen—who was fascinated by her lively manner. "His daughter and his wife," he confided to her, "were the two most wearisome queens he had ever met."

In spite of a keen interest in everything relating to the Court and to politics, Madame de la Ferté-Imbault could never be induced to enter Madame de Pompadour's circle, though she had known her in earlier days.

Madame d' Étioles had been introduced to Madame Geoffrin by Madame de Tencin— who already had the end to which she attained in view—and she soon ingratiated herself both with Madame Geoffrin and her daughter by her assiduous attentions and evident wish to please. A few years later she was known as the Marquise de Pompadour, and the most illustrious personages danced attendance upon the King's favourite who begged Madame de la Ferté-Imbault to accept some post near her at Court, but in vain. Her old friend always spoke well of Madame d' Étioles but she could never be persuaded to have relations with Madame de Pompadour.

Madame Geoffrin survived the illness which followed her attendance on the Jubilee a year, during which she was unable to move hand or foot with one exception when, by a supreme effort, she wrote the last words traced by her pen.

"I love you with all my heart." They were written to Poniatowski.

The report of this illness excited general regret abroad. Catherine, forgetful of her wrongs, remembered only their friendship, and suggested treatment and asked for news by every courier. Joseph II, visiting Paris, went to see her at her request. Her death occurred October 6th, 1777.

"I am very sorry for the death of Madame Geoffrin," wrote Catherine to Grimm.[1] "You will find a great void in Paris." And again: "I am not satisfied with the eulogies and 'portraits' of Madame Geoffrin, they all have the bourgeois look. One would believe them to have been written by the King of England, or by some *good citizen*, which is synonymous.[2]

[1] Oct. 29, 1777.   [2] Jan. 10, 1778.

The extravagant praises of the philosophers had, indeed, the appearance of being addressed to their benefactress rather than to the personality of Madame Geoffrin, and the brief sentence in which the Comtesse de la Marke told Gustavus III of the event gives a more just summary of the deprivation to society which her death entailed. " It is a loss for the arts and a good woman the less."

X

If we look for a moment at the inner workings of Madame Geoffrin's salon the reasons for her remarkable ascendency will soon be seen.

Her success was due to various causes. In the first place, of a bold, dominant nature she was naturally a leader of men. Then she possessed that practical intelligence which is always an element in success. Her salon was organised on business principles, she constantly applied herself to attain perfection in all its details and it was therefore the best administered of any salon. Extending over a period of thirty years its continuity added to its prestige and, amid the storms and uncertainty of the time, it represented permanency. Moderation, order, tranquillity—in spite of the Bohemian character of some of her guests— were the foundational and predominating notes of this famous salon.

It was not enough that an invitation should be sent a new-comer or that an habitué should be permitted to introduce a friend who, it was an unwritten law, should have some particular merit or métier, should be in fact a celebrity of some sort, but, once admitted, she bound him to her by the bonds of gratitude.

"The grass must not grow on friendship's path," was one of her characteristic sayings, and she continually practised this principle showering benefits, gifts, and attentions, according to their needs, on all those whom she patronised or wished to attach to her.

Not pretending to be a conversationalist herself she nevertheless skilfully led and directed the conversation in her salon. With over long stories she had no patience. One day at dinner observing a loquacious guest draw from his pocket a knife with which he proceeded to help himself, she drily remarked: "Monsieur le Comte, one must have long knives and short stories."

It will be seen that the leader of a salon followed a profession. For Madame Geoffrin, her rivals and her predecessors, their salons were the chief aims of their existence. To their direction all other occupations were entirely subordinated. They were quite truly kingdoms whose diverse elements must be harmonised, whose domains were strictly guarded, from whence unhappy exiles wandered, whose inhabitants sometimes deserted to the enemy, and which also sometimes received recruits from rival camps. They were governed after the manner of an absolute monarchy whose rule—and more particularly in the case of Madame Geoffrin was this true—was despotic and often tyranical; nevertheless the greatest artists submitted their work to her dictation who

was incapable of being a real judge of art,
and the most celebrated writers were anxious to have their productions approved by
this unlettered woman.

Faith in her judgment was well nigh universal. When Helvétius' *De l'Esprit* appeared, he exclaimed to his friends, " Let
us see how Madame Geoffrin will receive
me : it is only on consultation with this
thermometer of opinion that I shall know
exactly of the success of my work ! "

Madame Geoffrin did not possess the
forcible intellect of Madame Du Deffand, the
sensitive emotional nature of Julie de Lespinasse, nor was she, like Madame d'Épinay,
a writer. She does not represent the highest
order of mind. She was wanting in the
delicate shades of perception and of feeling. But all her friends felt that in Madame
Geoffrin they had a practical, a sagacious, and
a sure friend. She could hardly, however, be
called an ideal friend for, though she was
prepared to spare neither time, effort, nor
money to serve them, should misfortune
which she could not alleviate, befall, she

shut her eyes to their miseries and her ears to their complaints. In short, she put an end at once to any friendship which might prove painful and if a friend was separated from her as she thought forever, she schooled herself never to think of him again and refused to continue a correspondence with persons whose return was unlikely. If she entered a house and found it sad or gloomy she left it at once. She was ready to rejoice with those who were glad but not to weep with those who wept. That part of Christian doctrine she rejected from the beginning of her career.

The quality of common sense which Madame Geoffrin possessed in so large a degree was the virtue which she considered superior to any other and by its constant practice she became habituated to rigidly control, if not to altogether stifle, her impulses and emotions. The virtues she practised were not difficult ; she conformed to the Church to satisfy her ideas of propriety, law, and order ; she was charitable to satisfy instincts which nature had given her. Passion, excess in

C. A. HELVETIUS.

Né à Paris en Janvier 1715. Mort à Paris le 26 Décembre 1771.

HELVÉTIUS.
From an Engraving by St. Aubin, after the Portrait by Vanloo.

any form, was a danger to be avoided, and the passion of love or hate, of joy, or of grief, which deeper natures suffer or enjoy was unknown to her. She sought, at all hazards, to lead a tranquil life, at the expense, no doubt, of many finer feelings. It was always the voice of prudence to which she listened ; it was the watchword of this peace-loving, well-balanced, and disciplined nature. Therefore Madame Geoffrin had no absorbing emotional experiences, and she never made use of women's arts to attract the other sex. A slightly hard, cold, painfully polished product, she was never known to have melting moods. But she bound men to her by obligations such as practical help and by intelligent sympathy in their undertakings. Ambition was her only passion and, once admitted to this self-contained nature, it entered into full possession ; her husband, henceforth, was but a figurehead ; her daughter another impediment, another disappointment.

Madame Geoffrin presents a curious contrast of pride and modesty, of selfishness and generosity. The great causes for which her habitués were, for the most part, struggling, found her unresponsive and cold, her very morality in such an age proceeded, it might seem, rather from a cold nature and a calculating disposition, which always counted the cost, than from high ideals. Her reasonableness was carried to such a pitch as to be sometimes repugnant. One would wish to see higher aspirations, a heart more freely given to human affection, and with less thought of consequences. In fact one would like Madame Geoffrin to have been less sensible.

But such she was. If she made the most of her life who can say?

From the point of view of worldly wisdom there is no doubt as to the answer. An uneducated girl of common origin had lifted herself by her own unaided efforts to be a power in Europe. If she did not follow Emerson's mandate to " hitch your waggon to a star," she perhaps accomplished all that which lay within her scope. Eminently practical, she made good use of this talent ;

she lifted artists and musicians to a higher place in society than they had before occupied ; and her wide benevolence secured for her the esteem of every class of society. Critic, friend and patroness of artists, kindly and captious, generous and patronising, such is the figure which differentiates her salon from that of each of those women whose meetings, friends, joys, and troubles I have already attempted to outline. She is perhaps the most remarkable of any of them, presenting a curious study of the essentially bourgeois type tempered by the literary and artistic atmosphere of the times, never able, however, to throw off the native qualities of her character. The airs and graces which complete the portrait in Madame Du Deffand or Julie de Lespinasse sit as it were awkwardly on this sensible figure who in many respects resembles that of the literary ladies of London, such as Mrs. Thrale, rather than the more intellectual minds and more sensitive natures of the leading women of the age in France. She was as incapable of feeling the emotions which racked the ardent soul of

Julie de Lespinasse as she was of imitating the fine wit of Madame Du Deffand or of understanding the tender enthusiasms of Madame d'Épinay.

This excellent woman possessed the virtues and the failings of the bourgeoisie. Governed by common sense, illumined by the bright gleams of a generous nature, she demonstrates many of the drawbacks which result from a realistic conception of life. There were aims which she could not understand and such she deemed futile. The eighteenth century is marked in general by its limitations—as is the life of Madame Geoffrin. Her eyes were never lifted to the stars !

BIBLIOGRAPHY

The following are the principal works which have been consulted in the preparation of the preceding studies, and this list is for the use of those who may wish to pursue the subject in greater detail.

Aïssé. *Lettres portugaises avec les résponses; lettres de Mdlle. Aïssé,* etc., Paris, Bibliothèque Charpentier, 1873.

D'Alembert, *Œuvres,* Paris, Berlin, 1822, 5 vol.

Argenson, Marquis d', *Mémoires,* Publ., par R. d'-Argenson, 1825.

Barrière, M. F., *Bibliothèque des Mémoires relatifs à l'histoire de France pendant le XVIIIᵉ siècle avec avant-propos et notes.* Paris. Firmin-Didot et Cie., 1891.

Brunetière, M. Ferdinand, *Manuel de l' Histoire de la Littérature française,* Paris, Libraire Ch. Delagrave, 1907. *Les Philosophes et la Société Française.* Revue des Deux Mondes. Dec. 1, 1906.

Questions de Critiques, Paris, Calmann Lévy, 1889.

Choiseul, Le duc et la Duchesse de ; leur vie intime, leurs amis et leur temps. Par M. Gaston Maugras, 1902.

Choiseul, Le disgrace du duc et de la duchesse de ; la vie à Chanteloup, le retour à Paris, la mort. Par M. G. Maugras, 1903.

Du Deffand, Madame, *Correspondance complète de Madame Du Deffand avec la Duchesse de Choiseul, l'Abbé Barthélemy et Monsieur Craufort.* Publiée avec une introduction par Monsieur le Marquis de Sainte-Aulaire. Paris, Calmann Lévy, 1877, 4 vol.

Du Deffand, *Correspondance complète de la Marquise Du Deffand,* pub. par de Lescure, Paris, Plon, 1865, 2 vol.

Du Deffand, *Lettres de la Marquise Du Deffand à Horace Walpole,* Paris, chez Truettel et Wurtz, 1812, 4 vol.

Du Deffand, *Madame Du Deffand et sa Famille.* Par M. le Marquis de Ségur. Revue des Deux Mondes, 15 Nov., 1906.

Deschanels, M. Paul, *Figures de Femmes.* Paris, Calmann Lévy, 1889.

Diderot, *Correspondance de Diderot et de Mademoiselle Volland.* Paris, Garnier Frères, 1876.

Épinay, Madame d', *Mémoires.* Édition nouvelle et complète, avec une addition des notes et des éclaircissements inédits par M. Paul Boiteau. Paris, Bibliothèque Charpentier, 1891.

Épinay, Madame d', *Œuvres.* Avec une introduction par M. Challemel-Lacour. 2 Tomes. Tome I, *Lettres à mon fils.* Tome II, *Mes moments heureux.* Paris, Chez A. Santon, 1869.

Épinay, Madame d', *L'Amitié de deux jolies Femmes. Un rêve de Mlle. Clairon.* Publiés par Maurice Tourneux. Paris, Libra rie des Bibliophiles, 1885.

Épinay, Madame d', *Les Conversations d'Émilie.* 2 Tomes. Lausanne, 1784.

Épinay, Madame d', *La Jeunesse de Madame d' Épinay*. D' Après des lettres et des documents inédits. Par Lucien Pérey et Gaston Maugras. Paris, Calmann Lévy, 1898.

Épinay, Madame d', *Dernières Années de Madame d'Épinay*. *Son salon et ses amies*. D'Après des lettres et des documents inédits. Par Lucien Pérey et Gaston Maugras. Paris, Calmann Lévy, 1894.

Galiani, L'abbé, *Lettres de l'Abbé Galiani à Madame d' Épinay, etc.* Par Eugène Asse. Paris, Bibliothèque Charpentier, 1881.

Geoffrin, Madame, *Le Royaume de la rue Saint Honoré*. Par Pierre de Ségur. Paris, Calmann Lévy 1898.

Geoffrin, Madame, *La Correspondance inédite du Roi de Pologne, Stanislas Auguste Poniatowski et Madame Geoffrin*. Par le Comte de Mouy, 1875.

Goncourt, Edmond et Jules de, *La Femme au Dix-Huitième Siècle*. Paris, Bibliothèque Charpentier, 1901.

Grimm, Baron de, *Correspondance Littéraire, Philosophique et Critique du Baron de Grimm et de Diderot, Raynal, etc., publiée par Maurice Tourneux*, Paris, Garnier Frères, 1877 (16 vols.).

Grimm, Baron de, *Correspondance, etc.*, 1812, 1813, 1814, 17 vols. *en 3 parties*.

Hénault, *Mémoires du Président Hénault*. Rec. par le Baron de Vigan. Paris, 1855.

Hénault, *Le Président Hénault et Madame Du Deffand*. Par L. Pérey. Paris, Calmann Lévy, 1893.

Hénault, *Un Magistrat homme de lettres au XVIIIe siècle; le président Hénault, 1685–1770; sa vie, ses œuvres, 1903*. Par M. Henri Lion.

Houdetot, La Comtesse d', *Une amie de J.-J. Rousseau*. Par Hyppolyte Buffenoir. Paris, Calmann Lévy, 1901.

Hume, David, *Life and Correspondence of David Hume.* By J. Hill Burton, London, 1846.

Hume, David, *Letters of Eminent Persons addressed to David Hume.* 1849.

La Harpe, Jean François de, *Correspondance Littéraire, 1804-7.*

Lauzun, le Duc de, *Le Duc de Lauzun et la Cour Intime de Louis XV.* Par Gaston Maugras, Plon-Nourrit et Cie. Paris, 1900.

Lescure, M. F. A. de, *Mémoires biographiques et littéraires avec Introd. et Notes,* 1881.

Lespinasse, *Correspondance entre Mademoiselle de Lespinasse et le Comte de Guibert.* Par le Comte de Villeneuve-Guibert. Paris, Calmann Lévy, 1906.

Lespinasse, *Julie de Lespinasse.* Marquis de Ségur. Paris, Calmann Lévy, 1906.

Lespinasse, *Lettres de Mademoiselle de Lespinasse.* Par Eugène Asse. Paris, Bibliothèque Charpentier, 1876.

Lespinasse, *Lettres inédiles de Mademoiselle de Lespinasse à Condorcet, à d'Alembert, à Guibert et au Comte de Crillon.* Publiées par M. Charles Henry. Paris, E. Dentu, 1887.

Lespinasse, Mademoiselle de, *Mademoiselle de Lespinasse et la Marquise Du Deffand, suivi de documents inédits sur Mademoiselle de Lespinasse.* Par Eugène Asse, Paris. G. Charpentier, 1877.

Levis, Pierre Marc Gaston, Duke de, *Souvenirs et Portraits, 1780-1789,* Paris et Londres, 1813.

Marmontel, *Mémoires.* Par Maurice Tourneux. Paris, Librairie des Bibliophiles, 3 t. 1891.

Necker, Madame, *Le Salon de Madame Necker.* Par le vicomte d' Haussonville, Paris, 1882.

Necker, Madame, *Mélanges*. Paris, 1793.

Necker, Madame, *Nouveaux Mélanges*. Paris, 1801.

Rousseau, J.-J., *Julie ou La Nouvelle Heloïse*. Paris, Garnier Frères.

Rousseau, *Jean-Jacques Rousseau*. Jules Lemaitre, Paris, Calmann Lévy, 1907.

Rousseau, J.-J. *A New Study in Criticism*. By Frederika Macdonald. London, Chapman & Hall, 1906. New York, G. P. Putnam's Sons, 1907.

Roustan, M. Marius, *Les Philosophes et la société française au XVIIIᵉ siècle;* Lyon, chez Rey, et Paris, chez Picard et fils, 1906. Annales de l'Université de Lyon.

Sainte-Beuve, C. A., *Causeries de Lundi*. Paris, Garnier Frères, 1850.

Scherer, Edmond, *Études sur la Littérature Contemporaine*. Paris, Calmann Lévy, 1885.

Ségur, Pierre de, *Le Royaume de la rue Saint-Honoré*. Paris, Calmann Lévy, 1898.

Ségur, Pierre, de, *Julie de Lespinasse*. Paris, Calmann Lévy, 1906.

Staal, Marg. Jeanne de Launay, baronne de, *Mémoires,* Michaud et Poujoulet, Nouv. Coll., Series III, t. 10, 1850.

Suard, Madame, *Essais de Mémoires sur M. Suard*. Paris, Didot, 1820.

Tornézy, M., *Un bureau d'esprit au XVIIIᵉ siècle. Le Salon de Madame Geoffrin*. Lecêne et Oudin, Paris, 1895.

Walpole, Horace, *Letters of Horace Walpole*. Ed. by Mrs. Toynbee, 1905.

Weiss, J. J., *Essais sur l'Histoire de la Littérature française*. Paris, Calmann Lévy, 1891.

INDEX